THE PURPOSE OF MY LIFE:

NOW, THEN, AND IN THE FUTURE

Doreen McKenzie

ISBN: 9798739237934

Humanity –

- ❖ The Purpose of Life
- ❖ Reconciliation of Dawn
- ❖ A White Privilege
- ❖ Demands
- ❖ The Knee
- ❖ Dancing in the Streets
- ❖ Protests
- ❖ The Stakes
- ❖ Visibility at Last

THE PURPOSE OF MY LIFE

What was the purpose of my life?
Was it to heal or to cause more strife?
Why me and not all the others?
They too might have called out for their mothers.

What was the purpose of my life?
Was it to highlight the injustices that are so rife?
Was it to heal past wrongs that were done,
When so many black lives were taken by the gun?

What was the purpose of my life?
Was it to ensure others don't have to pay the price?
Let us face the truth that we can clearly see
Many other Georges have perished before me.

What was the purpose of my life?
Was it to watch the world unite?
Was I the one that the Almighty had chosen,
To expose how the hearts of some men are frozen?

What was the purpose of my life?
Was it because God chose me to expose their lies?
We were the first people on God's earth
And from our genes other nations were birth.

What was the purpose of my life? what is the answer?
Was it to make people stand up to the self-appointed masters?

Racism, prejudice and violence against black people in so many places
Despite the fact we are one human race but with different coloured faces.

What was the purpose of my life?
Why was I chosen as the sacrifice?
God in his wisdom allowed the world to see
How brutally and senselessly my life was taken from me.

What was the purpose of my life?
Was it to watch the whole world ignite?
With my neck pressed below his knee
Was this the catalyst to set people free?

The world has woken up to acknowledge the pain
That black people have had to endure as they are burdened under all the strain
Whatever we do it is never right
The white man is there always showing his might.

To show solidarity and stand up for what is right
Was the purpose of my life to lead the world towards the light?
To expose man's inhumanity to man and get decent people to understand
It is not the colour of your skin that matters
Myths of superiority and inferiority they must shatter
To unite the world and end racial strife
That was the purpose of my life!

RECONCILIATION AND A NEW DAWN

America is a country very divided
Despite the fact that she has people from many nations
Unfortunately, justice and fair play often seem so one sided
And those in power refuse to see and often dispute its causation.

Heavy policing which appeared to be the norm
Was miraculously absent when the Capital was stormed
Black Lives Matter protests were brutally crushed
By the police and army who were extremely robust.

However, we witnessed the double standard
Which left many people upset and angered,
When militia from all over the United States assembled
Rioters, looters and gangsters they resembled.

These people were able to gain entrance through gates
Which were supposed to be secure but were broken through by
people fuelled with hate
Having gained entrance, they were barely thwarted
As they roamed from room to room and continued spewing their
theories which were grossly distorted.

Through the actions of the protesters, and the inaction of the
police
Four people who were amongst the crowds, are now deceased.
Things were allowed to get out of hand
Because police and soldiers alike, refused to take a stand.

An election was won whether by fair means or foul
And a nation divided must now search its own soul
They must decide whether to look forwards or backwards
To make the right decision, they must weigh up many factors.

There is now a new President and a new Vice President
And on rebuilding and reuniting the nation is their sincere intent
Joe Biden is calling for peace and unity
In a nation that has been fed lies and encouraged to break the law
with impunity.
They have a tremendous job on their hands
To bring justice, healing and reconciliation to a very broken land.

Kamala Harris has a lot of credentials
Which have many unifying potentials
Her whole family unit is like the United Nations
As there are many nationalities who are her relations.
What better example is there of the possibility
That all the different peoples in America could become one entity.

A woman who is looked upon as a first
A position which could be either a blessing or a curse
Kamala, the eyes of the world will be resting on you
They will scrutinise and make their own interpretation of
everything you say and/or do.

A lot of expectations will be resting on your shoulders
Whilst for some others, their distrust and resentment slowly
smoulder
The road ahead will definitely not be easy
This is not a position in which one can be blithe and breezy.

But the toil and struggles of black heroes and sheroes who have
gone before
Have paved the way for you Kamala, to enable you and assist you
in opening many a door
On their shoulders you can proudly stand
I am certain your ancestors will see it as their honour and duty to
hold your hand.

Vice President Kamala, a lot is expected of you
Because that position you hold, is seen as quite a coup
There are people who wish you well and admire you by the score
And their elation can be evidenced worldwide from shore to
shore.

You are a woman of diverse pedigree
On this extraordinary road of making history
Your parents who are from different parts of the world
May not have believed your destiny, even if they had been told.

To be an immigrant in a foreign country
Comes with privileges but also has many boundaries
They both had to work very hard in their posts
To ensure that they reach their respective goals
You were brought up to have pride and determination
Which is evident to most people throughout the nation.

Your language and your standing are regarded with pride
As your background and ethnicity, you've never tried to hide
The relationship between your parents was not sustainable
But relationships are complex and that's quite understandable.

Being different does not appear to cause you any distress
With your current family structure many are impressed
You appear to have embraced the role of step mother
Giving children your love and care freely, and without too much
bother.

Your husband and in-laws are undoubtedly Jewish
And anyone who disputes your multi- cultural and multi-racial
family structure would be extremely foolish.

You hold the key for a reconciled nation
By the example of your strong and positive family union
You have shown the world that if different people unite
Love and light could prevail, and we could win any fight
Against hatred, bigotry and division
By putting aside our differences and come together as one.

Not everyone is the same but that does not mean that some people
are superior whilst others are inferior
What is seen on the outside only shows the exterior
We can learn to accept and embrace our differences
Whilst still acknowledging that we have our own special and
unique preferences.

South Asia is proud of the product of one of their daughters
And the people of the Caribbean feel the same because of your
father
There are pictures of you with both sides of your family
And the world can see that there's little or no animosity
In your esteemed position there's a lot of expectations

Don't be surprised if many are expecting and looking for perfection.

Kamala you acknowledged all the black people in America
Who came out and supported you from Illinois to Florida
You are prominent in a country that is widely divided
But you are the hope for a country which could eventually become more united
You mentioned that you have roots in the Caribbean
And you have shown your pride of also being South Asian.

Vice President Kamala many eyes all over the world are on you
To see if you actually achieve what you've set out to do
Some of the expectations will be very unreal
And lots of disappointments and pressures you will feel.

We've seen you dance and laugh and here's the deal breaker
You'll come through it all because you're the descendant of a
people from an island with very strong character.

Many ambitious young girls and young women will see you as a great example
Of what they can achieve in their lives, as they strive to reach the pinnacle
Especially people of colour who've often had their hopes and aspirations dashed
Because of the lack of privilege, opportunity, and racial barriers, which have held them back.
They are rooting for you to be the most successful Vice President
For that they are praying as you set this extremely high precedent.

You hold the hopes and the dreams of many who see your lineage
and who have goals for which they too aspire
They would like to express their love, admire and respect for you,
as a descendant of that most beautiful island of Jamaica.

WHITE PRIVILEGE

You are confused by my meaning of white privilege
And I am confused by your confusion
As usual I have to be your teacher
So here are a few examples which should make things much
clearer.

White privilege is when it is you who are constantly in the
position of power
While for me to reach such a position it's like trying to climb the
ivory tower.

Your white privilege connects you to people of power
Whilst when I'm stopped, I just have to cower
White privilege is when you can go anywhere
And don't feel any trepidation and immense fear.

White privilege is when you see a policeman coming towards you,
and you feel no panic because you know that you're not in danger
of being killed
Whereas I'm immediately seen as a threat and my entire being
with immense dread and fear is filled.

White privilege is when a white woman can weaponize the police
by calling them on an innocent unarmed black man
Knowing full well that he will end up looking down the barrel of a
gun.

White privilege is when you can drive a really top of the range expensive car and be perceived as the rightful owner
Unlike me who would be suspected of only being able to purchase this type of car because I'm either a thief or a drug dealer.

White privilege is when you and I commit the same crime
And you are set free whilst I am made to do time.

White privilege is when someone who looks like you commit a crime and you feel no responsibility nor feel that you will be blamed
Unlike me who knows that I will be judged and racially profiled because of my colour if the perpetrator and I look the same.

White privilege is when you go to a church and commit murder
And instead of taking you straight to prison, the police give you a drink and take you for a burger.

White privilege is when you are held on suspicion of committing double murder
And you have your injuries attended to and you're given water.

White privilege is when you get a traffic stop and you can reach in your pocket for your ID
But when I try to do the same, I'm shouted at and told to show my hands by a policeman with a gun pointing at me.

White privilege is when you and I are held as a suspect
I'm dehumanised whilst you are treated with respect.

White privilege is when you're in the classroom and it is
automatically assumed you know the answer
Whereas even though my hand shoots up, I'm constantly ignored
by the teacher.

White privilege is even as children when you and I have a fight
I am always in the wrong whilst you're automatically deemed to
be in the right.

White privilege is when as two school boys we both misbehave
I'm expelled from school whilst you are free to remain.

White privilege again in school is when you are perceived as
highly intelligent
Whereas I'm seen as a fool with very little or no intellect.

White privilege is when something goes down on the street and
we are both stopped
Little attention is paid to you whilst I'm immediately handcuffed.

White privilege is when we say the same thing and your voice is
heard
Whilst my voice gets drowned out or is totally ignored.

And let's not talk about higher education
Where I have to work twice as hard to get the same qualifications.

When I go for a job for which I know I'm highly qualified
With little or no qualifications your white privilege secures you
the job and that is not justified.

White privilege is when despite my many academic achievements
My progress is systematically blocked to prevent me to get into management.

And if by some miracle I secure the same job as you
I'm invariably paid less despite the fact that it's the same work we do.

And when you want to pretend you embrace diversity
Your white privilege enables you to hire me as a token to stop deeper scrutiny.

And when your sister or your daughter makes a pass at me
I am the one thought to be in the wrong, I am the one that the bigots see.

White privilege allows you to sleep when our children go out to socialise
Whilst I lay awake and worry if the police will allow my children to return home alive.

White privilege is when you can live wherever you please
Whilst I cannot do that because my colour causes unease.

White privilege is when you can wear a mask and not fret
But when I do the same, I am arrested because I am seen as posing a threat.

White privilege is when you can protest with your guns
But I with my bare hands am chased with tear gas, rubber bullets or batons.

White privilege is when we are both taken to court
You are presumed innocent until proven guilty, whilst I am
immediately assumed to be guilty, which is the reverse.

White privilege is when we are both committed to prison and we
do time
Your sentence is invariably much lighter than mine.

White privilege is when you can sit in a cafe or restaurant as long
as you like
Whilst when I try to do the same the police are called because I
don't have that right.

White privilege is when you can sell cigarettes on the street
Without any fear that police harassment or even your death you
could meet.

White privilege is when you can challenge without fear
When I do the same, I'm told I have a chip on my shoulder and
anyway, no one cares.

Consistent ill health and adverse poverty remains my portion
Which is something because of your white privilege you will
never have a notion.

The black man's life experience is so far from yours
Of that your white privilege consistently makes sure.

What is white privilege? I could go on and on
But suffice it to say, you've had your white privilege from the day
you were born.

So, having given you a snapshot of my life and my reality
I hope you will understand how this affects me and my family.

Now that you're more aware through your new found knowledge
Please start treating me right by giving up some of your white
privilege.

DEMANDS

Systematic exclusion and discrimination
Have been prevalent in many a nation.
But thank goodness there is a new energy about
Demanding justice and equality as generations of people continue
to shout.

Nations and governments have to be honest
So that people can have confidence to stop their protests.
Violence and intimidation seem to be the order of the day
But change must come, that's what we all say.

There has been systemic denial of opportunity
In jobs and positions that should be mandatory.
Black people now have an expectation of success
So your racism and prejudice we're demanding you address.

Many recommendations have already been made
And yet things continue to be the same.
The time for talking is over - we're tired of asking
Action is what we're now demanding.

We need to see evidence of intent
And proper recognition of our many achievements.
We're tired of being punished for showing assertiveness
We stand courageous in the face of sustained harassment.

Black people have always been rewarded for servility
But this should no longer be our young people's reality.

We demand a stop to racial discrimination
Which stops us from reaching our goals and meeting our
aspirations.

We want to be given the same opportunity
In jobs, wages, education including attendance at university.
We are not asking for special treatment
And we don't want tokenism or to be used as an experiment.

This will continue to be an uncompromising fight
So stop prevaricating and do what is right.
Equality in everything should be mandatory
No more lame excuses for differences and disparity.

There is now universal acclaim
For what has gone on before to change.
We don't mind being separate but we must be equal
No more excuses and no more denial.

There is a weariness in constantly being marginalised
There is no longer room for compromise.
We will not be held responsible for any consequence
So those of you in positions of power please use your influence.

We hope to see an end to this confrontation
As you recognise and honour our contributions.
Stop the talking and act with integrity
We're demanding equality and not charity.

And whilst we're at it, let us remember this
Kind thoughts and friendly actions are priceless.

Even though for past deeds you owe us compensation
That fight we are parking for another occasion.

We have seen the fight from many weary people diminished
Even though they're highly qualified and distinguished.
This generation will take no more mocking
Because for changes and opportunities we are flocking.

As we anticipate your long-awaited actions
Remember it's what we deserve with no more sanctions.
So we hope you won't find it too hard
To stop considering and act, by meeting our demands.

THE KNEE

To show my solidarity I get down on my knee
Because I cannot understand the hopelessness I see
It is not a comfortable stance to take
But I have to take a stand for decency and democracy's sake.

I understand that things will have to change
And I can only do what is within my range
I know that if I continue to stay quiet
It is something I will always regret.

'Burn baby burn' was a cry I heard in the past
Black Lives Matter is the uniting cry at last
A slogan saying 'all lives matter' is just a distraction
We need a unifying cry that will shake the administration.

There is no going back we need to go forward
I know there's a lot of fear that we're going to lose power
But unless we accept that the system is broken
We will continue to use the odd black person as a token.

I want to stop being part of the problem
Because my silence makes it look as if I'm one of them
I realise that going on my knees is not enough
I need to share my privilege; I now realise that I have way too
much.

The beneficiaries of privilege refuse to give it up
And that's from the lowliest to the ones at the top

If I continue to keep silent and don't make a fuss
Then I'm just as guilty as those who call themselves boss.

Fair Education and good job opportunities are denied a section of
the population
We use them to do the work that has no chance of promotion
And even when they work hard to break the social and racial
barrier
They're still not accepted because we continue to look at them as
being inferior.

Well as from today I want to be part of the solution
Equal treatment for all must no longer for some be an illusion
The privileges which I so freely enjoy
Will from this day onwards be available to all.

Up until now I've been part of the problem
It takes a nation's rage to make me own up to them
I always said that I was not a racist
But marching and rioting forces me to examine my attitude and
confront this.

I've scrutinised my life and the things I hold dear
And recognise my part and has confronted my fear
So the sight of me being on my knee
Is not a token, this is the beginning of the new me.

DANCING IN THE STREET

You were ordered out with your guns, the protesters to defeat
But instead of shooting them down, you danced with them in the
streets
It was so heart-warming to evidence
Some members of the military sticking two fingers up at the
president.

Your common sense and humanistic approach
Were most appreciated and beyond reproach
By your calm and considerate action
You helped to bring healing to a nation.

Had you gone in with all guns blazing
And did not pay heed to your military training
You could have made a bad situation so much worse
And taken the whole reason for the protest off its course.

Calling out the military was a sign of desperation
By a president who had his sights set on re-election
But the military acted in good faith
And were responsible for bringing calmness to the state.

Admittedly at times there was a lot of confusion
As there was no sense that the military was not in collusion
With a system that wanted them to act tough
And put many of the young people in handcuffs.

But because of your calm composure and general stance
Purpose and confidence, you helped to enhance
The atmosphere changed and the marchers were emboldened
To continue with their march and display the banners they were
holding.

They felt their actions were vindicated
And their determination and spirits were invigorated
They now felt more relaxed and quite inspired
When they realised that not one bullet would be fired.

The military were professional and kind
And their intention they did nothing to hide
As they lined up along the street
And surprised the protesters by taking a backseat.

No violence or intimidation did they promote
And the protesters were determined no conflict to provoke
When they came face to face with each other, there seemed to be
shown mutual respect
Which was what was hoped for but they did not really know what
to expect.

The military did not appear to feel threatened and they were
unfazed
As upon the huge crowds of protesters they gazed
Several of them broke rank and took a protester's hand
The gesture was appreciated- maybe it was planned.

What could have been a very tricky situation
Turned out to be something that touched the entire nation

As the protesters were able to assemble and march in peace
With their chanting and banners the entire world they managed to
reach.

The stance the military took was truly inspirational
And their behaviour was seen as truly sensational
So thanks to the soldiers, the marchers had no need to retreat
As military personnel and protesters danced in the streets!

PROTESTS

You might very well not agree with me
I don't expect you to see exactly what I see
It is my right to protest in my way
And how I choose to do this, you certainly have no say.

It is impossible for you to understand how I feel
When I decide that my action, is to kneel
I could have gone wild, and caused a riot or loot
But that would have brought the whole movement into disrepute.

You have your own agenda, of that I am sure
And sadly, I realise that your position is far from pure
Because of your high profile and your privilege
That does not give you the right, my intentions and actions, to pillage.

How I choose to show my discontent
Whether with a low profile or very prominent
Is a decision I alone can take
And do it in such a way, as to make no mistake.

The fact that you don't like what I do
Does not bother me, though it might bother a few
You feel that you must pander to a certain section
And the name I have for people like you, I just cannot mention.

I have every right to express my feelings
Especially as it's with people like you that I'm dealing

Taking the knee or raising a fist
Are actions I will take, and will never desist.

So you can do all the talking you like
I can even supply you with a mike
Your views and opinions are yours and not mine
And there are many who will agree with me, you will find.

So despite what you think and what you're expressing
Your views will not have my head spinning or reeling
I will continue with my chosen form of protesting
Even though my patience, you're sorely testing.

Some people's lives have never been great
Where they are born or the colour of their skin, at times
immediately seals their fate
The truth of the matter is that you'll never understand what it's
like
When your whole existence is under attack.

We all have to find ways of dealing with our limitations
Without experiencing too much stress or frustration
So please get off your high horse and try to see things from other
people's points of view
Not everyone feels the need to deny their roots, like you.

Can I therefore ask you please to desist
From giving a point of view which everyone should resist
I will raise my fist, take the knee or wave my placard
Seeing the amount of people who agree with me, will always be
my reward.

It is clear that you have no empathy
And therefore, you cannot show sympathy
You will never stop me from exercising my right to protest in a
visible way
So keep your opinion, I'm not interested, even if it causes you
dismay!

No one should spend their entire life feeling defeated or
marginalised
So for my actions I will never apologise
Today the spotlight is on me and mine
But be warned, because tomorrow or the day after, it could be on
you and yours, that the bright light of hate will shine!

THE STAKES

Why are you asking me why I take to the streets?
What did you say? Am I not afraid of defeat?
We marched and sang all through the sixties
Seeking an end to our daily miseries.

Peaceful marches proclaiming 'we have a dream'
Hoping to see an end to being treated so mean
We marched and sang 'we shall overcome'
But forty years later that battle is still not won.

What are you asking me? Am I a rioter?
Excuse me? You think we should be quieter?
Rioting is the only thing these people will understand
That's the only way I know to take the power out of their hands.

How dare you label me a looter
Why don't you go and harass the shooter?
I only take the things I need
Because I was brought up never to steal.

Looting, stealing - what is the difference?
The difference is having the means and the affluence
I'm tired of seeing rich people in their expensive clothes
Whilst my poverty holds me in a bind of cheap robes.

And you - why are you setting fires?
Are you one of those that the agitators have hired?
Are you genuinely protesting for change

Or are you just here because of your age?

My age? What is the significance of my age?
No one is either too young or too old to feel the rage
The financial gap between blacks and whites
Is just one of the reasons we must unite and fight.

These countries were built on black oppression
Although I'm in poverty stealing was not my intention
But in order for there to be meaningful change
The beneficiaries of privilege must also feel my outrage.

Without meaningful change there will be no justice
And without justice there will be no peace
This is my message and there should be no illusion
Rioting, looting and burning is our fight for inclusion.

If my actions make you uncomfortable
Come and let us sit around the table
Those with their privileges must not persist
All we want is an equal chance to coexist.

The stake is high after 400 years of dominance and oppression
This can only be broken down with love and compassion
Like you we demand Life, liberty and the pursuit of happiness
That's all we are seeking, and will settle for nothing less!

VISIBILITY AT LAST

Black people have striven for centuries to be acknowledged and
recognised
For their many inventions and contributions which have been
compromised
They have never been given a voice nor an acknowledgement of
their many sacrifices
But the time has come when they must take charge of their own
destiny and be much more decisive.

Today's generation is standing on the shoulders of many heroes
and sheroes who have gone before
Many names we have forgotten, and many we have never known.
One love, one heart, is a very good way to start
Unity is what we have to forge, if we want to stand a chance.

Harriet Tubman started to pave the way
With her strength and her vision for freedom, she invented the
underground railway
Nanny of the Maroons fought the British army
With her organising skills and her quest for Liberty.

Marcus Garvey, with his hopes and his dreams
Tried to realise these with the establishment of the Black Star
Shipping Company
Martin Luther King organised the peaceful marches
Because he had a dream, from which he would not be thwarted.

Mary Seacole made her own way to the battlefield during the
Crimean war
When she offered her services as a nurse, she was not accepted
because of a colour bar.

Rosa Parks, broke the rules and sat down on the bus
She knew there would be repercussions, she knew there would
have been an almighty fuss.

Nelson Mandela spent almost a lifetime in prison, most of it in
solitary confinement
He came out oozing charisma, without bitterness but a
determination to reconcile all the different political fragments.

Barack Obama became president of the United States of America
The heroes that went before him predicted that a Black man would
work hard for such an honour.

But despite the fact that his presidency was fraught with
disappointments and frustrations
He kept his cool, and demonstrated to all, that he was truly a
dignified statesman.

Many of our ancestors refused to be broken under the lash
Despite the fact that many careful plans were very often smashed.

They were beaten, they were chained, even branded but they
continued to try
Even though they were aware that if they were found out they
would possibly die.
Their quest for freedom and humanity, was plain for all to see

They ran away, had their feet cut off but they still maintained their dignity.

For 400 years our ancestors were held captive, turned into slaves and broke their backs
Stolen, kidnapped, shackled, transported and exchanged for cash.
Families were separated as members were killed or sold
But that did not stop them standing up to their tormentors through all their suffering they continued to be bold.
They were forbidden to speak their own language so they could not communicate
But their intelligence was underestimated, despite the fact they could not congregate.

Our resilient, brave determined ancestors, found ways to speak to each other
They invented looks, signs and songs, which cemented them together.
They were able to make their pact
When any of them came under attack.
Dear ancestors, you have served as an example
And it's our responsibility to honour you and carry on the mantle.

The pain, humility and suffering our ancestors bore is really hard to imagine
But we know they had put up a good fight, so that we can go on living.

Future generations need to know that we have been left a great legacy

It is really up to all of us to build on this, so that we can determine our own destiny.

Many black men, women and children, have been murdered throughout the world
Most have gone unrecognised and their stories have never been told.

Then we saw a picture of George Floyd with a knee pressing on his neck
And the image was so disturbing that it made the whole world sit up and take a reality check.

They looked at their own attitudes, their unconscious bias and racial injustice
And decided that this cannot continue, they have to act, and stamp out discrimination, racism and prejudice.

All of a sudden Black Lives Matter
And the myths and misconceptions are being shattered.
At one time we were definitely invisible
Our images on any advert or most programmes, were not seen as suitable.
But now as soon as you turn on your TV
All children can see people looking just like you and me.

We are no longer solely being portrayed as the prostitute, the drug pusher, or the thug
But are featured as responsible people who are involved in all walks of life, so hopefully those negative images will no longer be plugged.

Martin Luther King marched so that we can walk
Rosa Parks sat, so that we can stand tall
Nanny fought, so that we can be free
Although we are still struggling for true freedom and equality.

As we stand on your shoulders, we say thank you all for the great
sacrifices you made
So that we can go about our daily lives, without always being too
afraid.
We are not saying that everything is fair, and we do not still have
to fight
But you went on before us, and we are travelling in your light.

There is still an awful lot left to be achieved
And people the world over have woken up, and are determined to
believe.
That because of the trailblazers that our ancestors became
Their names and their achievements will always be revered and
claimed.

We will no longer sit and expect others to fight our battles
But will get up and stand up for our rights to no longer be treated
like chattels.
The momentum of this current movement is intended to improve
lives
And for equal treatment and inclusion we will continue to strive.
We revere you, and honour you, dear ancestors because you gave
your lives so unselfishly
To make sure that your descendants are treated with dignity, as we
are now at last afforded some visibility.

The Eaves of Emotion-

- ❖ Loss and Grief
- ❖ The Universal Language
- ❖ The Smile
- ❖ Eavesdropping
- ❖ The Race
- ❖ The Truth of the Photograph
- ❖ The Scammer
- ❖ Family Feud
- ❖ The Dream

LOSS AND GRIEF

Life is filled with both darkness and light
And we owe it to ourselves to live a good life
Many loved ones have not managed to live out their dreams
Life can be a bitch, or at least sometimes that's how it seems.

We've all lost dear loved ones, some not so long ago
And have had to deal with immense sorrow and woe
But I'm hopeful that they're all dancing around the throne
As their dear departed souls have been called back home.

We are made to believe that your hearing is the last sense to go
So, as we whispered words of love, we sincerely wished you to
know
That despite the fact that you will be out of our sight
Your place will remain in our hearts, as that was your right.

Some loved ones passing we were not able to share
We were unable to be near but we hope they knew that we truly
cared
What your last moments were like we do not know
But we hope you had someone with you as on your last journey
you go.

Your life with us has been truly remarkable
Your contribution to our existence makes your memories sparkle
You were not created to spend too long on earth
But your influence and achievements have proclaimed your worth.

You are truly missed and that's for sure
We look for you every time we come through the door
Your photographs which are still on the shelf
We often take down and hold against ourselves.

Memories of you are all around
Everyday new thoughts of you resound
Your voice, your smile, your unique laughter
Brings sadness as well as incredible joy, which nothing can
shatter.

We will go through the five stages of grief
And going through them, will eventually bring us great relief
We need to accept that grieving is a necessary process
Which does not always leave us feeling bereft.

It is impossible to experience loss without suffering grief
But that is ok, because it helps to strengthen our beliefs
That the cycle of life does not end with death
But it is often the beginning of deep emotions we need to address.

Grief allows us to acknowledge the importance of life
It gives us the chance to mend all old troubles and strife
Disagreements happen all too often
And this is our chance to both give, and receive pardon.

We must strive to live in harmony and peace
Mend old grievances, and cause frictions to cease
Use grief to teach you the profound love and reverence
You will miss when a loved one is no longer present.

Learn to live with love because life is fragile
Cherish every look, every word, every smile
Loss and grief brings wonderful memories and a realisation of
what we have loved and lost
And we can look back with gratitude knowing that what you
shared with us in life, will be revered at all cost.

Memories keeps one going in a positive way
It plants the seed of hope for calmer and better days
It helps us to open our eyes to another reality
And acknowledge that although life is good, we must embrace our
own mortality.

Everything happens for a reason
We know that when we observe the four seasons
Nature shows that most flowers and vegetation on earth
Goes through death before there is glorious regeneration and
rebirth.

So beloved family and friends who have gone on before
Please make a way for us, because of one thing we're sure
None of us were born to stay in this world forever
No matter how much we think we are great or clever.

So until we are all finally reunited
Although early demise we are not necessarily inviting
I feel confident our reunion will be joyous for sure
And our sense of incredible loss and grief, will be no more.

THE UNIVERSAL LANGUAGE

What is your idea of the universal language?
This question has caused many people anguish
But for me it is a very simple question
And I will break from the usual tradition
My universal language is food
It is something which nourishes and puts the whole world in a
good mood.

That would be great if everything was even
Many people go hungry sometimes for no obvious reason
The world is not an even playing field
Those who have a lot sometimes are very mean
For me the universal language is religion
People have a choice how they worship depending on what they
see as normal.

I strongly disagree with you
Religion is alright but this is my view
Many a war has been fought in the name of religion
And sometimes it has been hard to make a decision
The universal language in my opinion is laughter
Because laughter tends to transcend every border.

I'm inclined to disagree with you
Laughter is good but people shed tears too
Life tends to throw up issues which could be happy or sad
And we can only laugh when we are really glad
For me the universal language is love

It is a gift sent to us from our Father above.

Love is important in all our lives
It is what helps us to progress and strive
But sadly, being loved is not everyone's experience
Many people in their lives for love they've mourned the absence.

Everything you've said I certainly won't dismiss
But I really think you have all been remiss
The universal language transcends food, religion, laughter and
love
Although it embraces all the above
Despite the fact that you're lonely hungry or sad
One thing in this world makes everyone glad
It fills each soul with much delight
And helps one to forget their sorry plight
Music is the only thing with the ability
To help humans to forget their fragility
Even if it is only for a while
The sound of music energises and makes the saddest heart smile
For me there is definitely no contest
Whether you are just listening or dancing music is the best.

Music is the only thing that eases the heart, the body and the mind
It takes you on an infinite journey you will find
Music has the ability to soothe the troubled soul
And expose the goodness and magic even the most desperate
situation can hold
It relieves the heart and mind from real or perceived bondage
And because of that, music for me, is definitely the universal
language.

THE SMILE

A smile can always tell you someone's mood
That is if you're sensible and not easily fooled
I had such an interesting experience recently
Which I hope will not be happening with any frequency.

I was so full of joy with the fantastic news
That to my friend's house I practically flew
I really had to share what I had just been told
This information was too precious for me to hold.

I got to her house very eager to share
But when I excitedly imparted my news, she only stared
I was baffled by the reaction of my friend
This was definitely not how I thought our friendship would end.

I stilled my heart and tried again to tell my story
But as I started, she tossed her head and told me not to worry
She had heard me the first time so there was no need to repeat
I was so stunned I just stared at my feet.

I was about to turn and go back home
Her reaction had shaken me to my very bone
But she hugged me and began to smile
The smile was so insincere I wanted to run a mile.

I noted the movements of her lips
But the rest of her face remained very stiff
There was no light or brightness in her eyes

And the realisation of her feelings almost made me cry.

I went home feeling rather deflated
Wondering what kind of animosity, I could have created
I was so sure she would have been happy for me
But I should have known that no kind of reaction is ever guaranteed.

I waited a few more days before I told another friend
I was less exuberant as I did not want to offend
But she grabbed me in her excitement
And my confidence returned and my tension lightened.

Her genuine smile filled my heart with cheer
As I could see her grinning from ear to ear
And as she held me and hugged me tight
I was reassured that everything would be alright.

I was now emboldened to repeat my story
But was careful not to crown myself in glory
My third friend's smile was sweet and gentle
My success to her was something essential.

When my brother heard my story, although he was glad
The smile he gave me was somewhat sad
He knew that my ambition was to go abroad
And to achieve that goal I had worked very hard.

I reviewed the different reactions to my news
And felt both joy and sadness when I examined the clues
The smiles told me exactly what was in their hearts

There was no disguising their varying emotions and thoughts.

The jealous smile will just stay at the lips
And the coldness in the eyes will make your heart flip
The genuine smile lights up the whole face
Transmitting its joy all over the place.

The gentle warm smile also shows your news was well received
Their happiness for you is easily perceived
Even the sad smile imparts warmth and love from the start
Because the entire face especially the eyes expressed what is
really in the heart.

As can be seen a smile can convey so many different things to let
one know
When feelings of sadness, joy, pleasure, disappointment and even
envy a smile can show
Sad, disappointed and envious smiles make one uncomfortable
But a joyous smile is returned filled with enough gratitude to
make one feel humble.

So, whenever you have a story to share
The reaction of others you have to be aware
Be careful how you interpret a smile
As they can differ by as wide as a mile.

EAVESDROPPING

I was in the supermarket when I overheard the two women talking
One was answering the questions the other one was asking.
I slowed my pace so that I could listen
There was no part of that conversation I thought I should be
missing.

They were discussing what they had been doing
And commenting generally on how they've been feeling.
The conversation was intense and went on in this vane
And the more they talked, the more it appeared that they were
disillusioned and were full of disdain.

I felt like my whole life was on hold
Waiting for more information to unfold.
It is hard to describe how I was feeling
But I knew that my whole world was reeling.

Every day when the News is read
We hear about the amount of people who are dead.
But that does not mean that we should live in fear
Because every life whether past or present, is a person who is, or
was, held very dear.

I felt that this statement was my cue
I knew instantly what I had to do.
I approached the ladies with a lot of daring
They were not amused, they thought I was too interfering.

But I decided to stand my ground
As I timidly looked around.
I felt I needed them to hear me out
I preferred to speak softly but thought I might end up having to shout.

Why do you spend so much time listening to the News?
I wouldn't do that if I was in your shoes.
There is no need for all this doom and gloom
We have to make up our minds this situation will not be ending any time soon.

There is a lot of goodwill about
Neighbours are now willing to help each other out.
You can get up and go out for a walk
There's fresh air and lots of nature's wonders in the park.

There are lots of other programmes on the television
You just have to make the right decision.
To be entertained and to have a laugh
I really don't think that is too much to ask.

Can I also please give you another piece of advice
None of us have complete control over our lives.
The people who have died and have gone on before
Are still in our hearts even though we don't see them anymore.

No one will be in this world forever
So it is important that whilst we're here, our lives we should treasure.
We can always find something for which to be thankful

It is good to be encouraging, positive and mindful.

It all depends on your point of view
But even if you stay at home there's a lot that you can do.
Instead of looking at everything so negatively
Do yourself a favour and think more positively.

You had no right to interfere in our talk
But the points you've raised have certainly made their mark.
Keeping a positive attitude is extremely vital
For our general health and our ultimate survival.

I felt exonerated when I heard what one of the women had to say
Though the look from her companion made me realise that her
views would be harder to sway.
I felt the need to apologise and get on with my shopping
My remarks had made a difference despite the fact that they found
my interest in their conversation rather shocking.

I walked away knowing I had made a positive impression
And secretly hoped they would both act on my suggestions
So please understand how deep a conversation could get
When you interfere in people's business, whilst in the
supermarket.

THE RACE

I sauntered up to the starting line
I felt confident because I was young, fit and in my prime
I didn't even give the other competitors a glance
Because I knew they didn't stand a chance.

I exercised and stretched my muscles
I waved my arms and cracked my knuckles
I kicked my legs and limbered up
Because winning this race for me was a must.

I crouched down and put my hands on the ground
Just then I had the strangest urge to look around
I knew that would have been a stupid thing to do
But I felt compelled to take a glance or two.

I took a quick look to the left and then to the right
It was then I realised I had to run with all my might
My biggest rival was in lane two
And to stop him winning I knew what I had to do.

I heard the words "on your mark"
And realised that the race was about to start
If I was to put my plan into action
I only had a matter of a second.

We were now being told to get set
The palms of my hands began to sweat
Did I dare try to carry out my plan?

Would anyone notice my cunning sleight of hand?

I had to act quickly before I lost my nerve
But if I cheated what purpose would that serve?
Isn't it better to be an honest loser,
And accept my defeat like a good old trooper?

The instruction was now to get ready
And I had to get my nerves steady
Oh, my goodness what should I do
I began to panic and my mind was in a stew.

I only had seconds to make my decision
Whatever my action, it had to be done with precision
Did I have the time to make another quick glance?
Did I dare risk disqualification by taking that chance?

Go! I heard the word very clearly
Have I the ability to win this race fairly?
Everyone started to run
As they heard the sound of the gun.

Very soon I realised I was the only one running
I was fired up and the adrenaline was pumping
I had no idea whether I was at the front or the back
But I felt exhilarated as my feet pounded the track.

I ran as if this race was going to be my last
I know I'm a quick runner, I know I am fast
The finishing line was coming in sight
And I continued running with all my might.

As I reached the line I stumbled and fell
Had I crossed the line? it was hard to tell
I raised myself up on my hands and knees
Hoping that I had won with ease.

I felt sure I had not cheated
So even if in this race I was defeated
I could hold up my head with grace and pride
My conscience would be clear because I would have nothing to
hide.

What's that noise that I am hearing
Oh, how wonderful, it was people cheering
Wait a minute, the sound has become muffled
I felt confused and rather puzzled.

The noise had now become quite deafening
There was shouting which got louder as I was listening
Suddenly I jumped up with a leap
I now understand that I was asleep.

What are you doing in there? You will be late
I closed my eyes as I examined my fate
I rushed around to get myself ready
It was important to get my nerves steady.

I didn't even know that I was sleeping
And the race was on my mind so
I was dreaming
Come on, come on, my team mates were urging

As the knots in my stomach was twisting and turning.

We eventually reached the stadium
The crowd was going so crazy that I almost lost my equilibrium
As I nervously went to check my spot
And was really happy with the place I got.

The race has started, we are on our way
What position I will come, I cannot say
But whether I get first, second or third place
I'll be grateful that I didn't oversleep and miss the race.

TRUTH OF THE PHOTOGRAPH

It is said that the camera never lies
But sometimes I can hardly believe my eyes.
The man told me that he was a professional photographer
And he would create the perfect picture that I am after.

I dressed up in my Sunday best and went down to his studio
I diligently searched for the location but when I found it, I felt
very low.
The building looked so old and derelict
I wondered if this man was just playing a trick.

I turned and was about to retrace my steps
But changed my mind as a little doubt in my heart crept.
It is not good to be so judgemental
Let me just knock on the door and not be so regimental.

I plucked up my courage and knocked on the door
And it opened so quickly I was shaken to the core.
The spectacle that greeted me as I entered the room
Filled me with a lot of trepidation and gloom.

This place looked dingy and in need of some paint
And all the furnishing and decorations looked really quaint.
But the photographer directed me to his studio
And this space was so different it filled me with wonder.

The inside of the studio was a spectacle to behold
As bit by bit my eyes began to adjust to the wonders that unfold.

The room was beautifully decorated and was full of splendour
And I couldn't help but be suspicious and I began to wonder.

How could such a space exist in a derelict building
The sensation I was feeling was rather chilling.
Nonetheless because I was dressed in my Sunday best
I made up my mind that I had nothing to lose so I might as well
take the risk.

I posed for the photo, turning this way and that
As the photographer clicked away with me sitting on a chair and
sometimes on a mat.
I began to feel emboldened as the camera flashed
I couldn't wait to see the results as I grew more confident and
quite unabashed.

The photographer seemed to be an expert at his craft
So the more he clicked away I became relaxed and even managed
to laugh.
The session seemed to have been going on forever
But I knew that to get perfection I had to endeavour.

At last, I was told that the session was over
And to return in a couple of days when I will see the exposures.
I went away feeling relieved and excited
Because I felt sure that the photos would make me feel delighted.

The day of reckoning came all too soon
As I found myself back in that splendid room.
A whole portfolio was handed to me
So that I could take my time and go through it leisurely.

Oh, but my, who is this I am looking at
That surely can't be me, I look far too fat.
The splendid clothes that I was wearing
Looked washed out as if the colours were fading.

The eyes in the photograph looked big and cold
And my beautiful face looked haggard and old.
This surely must be a tremendous mistake
Please take this back and give me my photos for goodness sake.

There is no mistake those photos are you
They don't look too flattering that is true.
But you must believe that the camera is honest
To turn us into raving beauties it has never promised.

So I had a real hard decision to make
Should I pay for these images which seem hideous and real fakes.
Or should I politely make an excuse
As acknowledging this stranger I just had to refuse.

But the photographer had a trick or two up his sleeve
And he saw my confusion as I got up to leave.
He kindly patted me on my shoulder
As he handed me another folder.

I looked at him as I sat back down
And as I looked, I could feel myself frown.
Because in these photographs I could see
What I had imagined was the real me.

So now I am wondering what is the truth
The haggard fat old woman or this sprightly looking youth.
Which of these photographs is telling a lie?
What are these diverse images trying to imply?

The way we see ourselves and the way we are perceived
Sometimes it is hard to process and believe.
But I will content myself by thinking that beauty is in the eyes of the beholder
And might well have nothing to do with the images in either of these folders.

What is important is how you feel inside
Because inner beauty is impossible to hide.
So regardless of how the photography makes you look
Goodness, kindness and compassion extols people's beauty in my book.

SCAMMER

Run, run you have every reason to run
Run you old scammer, because you know what you have done
If you had not been discovered today
I wonder with how much of this behaviour, you've already got
away.

Run, run, because you have no heart
You have no care for people who genuinely have it hard,
Life can be tough if you're desperately poor
But people like you who already have enough, always want more.

Run, run, you great big cheat
I'm going to do all I can to make you feel the heat
What made me take such an interest in you, I really don't know
Maybe it was because you were driving, ever so slow.

Run, run, you're so very selfish
Do you realise you're doing many people out of a dish?
Your actions were furtive, you thought you were alone
Thank goodness I decided to pick up my phone.

Run, go on, run faster still
You could have done a deserving person out of a meal
Have you ever thought how your behaviour impacts?
Your action will badly affect others, and that's a fact.

Run, lady run but my suspicion arose
The minute I watched you put on your fake clothes

Rolling in the grass, was a touch of brilliance
Also putting on a wig to change your appearance.

Run, you go on and run
You thought you would have got away with that scam
There are people who are genuinely in need
But they will miss out because of your greed.

It was my duty to call you out
The minute I realised what you were about
There are people who would really like to help
Those who are in need, and do not have your wealth.

You came here driving in your lovely car
I have no idea whether you live in this neighbourhood, or if
you've come from afar
But be assured that this will be the last time you pull this stunt
So, I will tell you your fate, and I will be blunt.

There are many people who are genuinely in need
Who the general public would willingly feed,
But because of the actions of people like you who are not sincere
They are ignored because it is not believed they are really in
despair.

I will make sure the whole world sees your face
So that you cannot do this same scam in some other places
This is the day of reckoning for you, as I bring an end to what you
may see as fun
You will never be able to hide, so go on lady continue to RUN!

FAMILY FEUD

What is it you said to me? You want me to say it again?
You heard me the first time so don't bother to pretend
I'm not quite sure what you're doing here
Because when you should have, you showed no care
So don't come now with your crocodile tears
I know you've hardly visited over the years.

Do you really want to hear my mouth?
Do I need to scream and shout?
I've told you once and I'll tell you again
Move away from here and take your friend
What are you doing trying to come into the house?
I'm warning you; you'd better go as quietly as a mouse.

Just who do you think you are talking to
What gives you the right to try to tell me what to do
We are the next of kin and you are a stranger
You had better watch out or you could be in danger
Move out of my way and let me pass
This is the last time I'm going to ask.

What is all that noise? What's going on out there?
This is a house in mourning, or don't you care?
Ah, now I understand what is going on
What can I do for you, how can I help you young man?
No, you cannot barge your way inside
Are you not understanding that someone just recently died?

I know what you lot are trying to do
I'm sure I have more right, to be here than you
So, you're not going to dissuade me that's for sure
So please take yourself from in front of the door
I do not need to prove to anyone who I am
Stop trying to bar my way, you stupid old man.

At least I managed to live to be old
You'd better watch yourself before I knock you out cold
Although I'm old I'm still very strong
So, if you're thinking you can manage me you've got it
completely wrong
And who is that woman coming up by your right
With her face all screwed up like she's ready for a fight?

What's all that commotion outside at the gate
Why can't you all behave yourselves, don't you see it's getting
late?
The woman who lived here was very respectable
So please stop your noise, we don't want any trouble
I don't know who you are, I don't recognise you on sight
So please go away we're having a family and close friends nine
night.

And who might you be, are you family or friend?
We've not just turned up at a dead house, we're not following a
local trend
Our presence here is our right as we are very close family
members
And if you insist on keeping us out, I'm going to lose my temper
We have much more reason to be here than most of you I am sure

And if we need to prove it, I can do so, I'm not arguing any more.

Come on and prove to us who you are because we're not
admitting any strangers
The only people we are waiting on are the entertainers
People come to these events just to get food and drink
The fact that they are inconveniencing others, they don't bother to
think
Well, this is not a free for all people are here by invitation
You will only be allowed inside if you can prove you are a
relation.

Why do I have to prove to you who I really am?
Have you any idea how far we're coming from?
I have a document in my bag which will prove without a doubt
Our connection to the deceased we can truly vouch
So stop barring our way so that we can show you that you're
wrong
You will feel so ashamed of your stance when you realise we
belong.

Now that you're inside let us see what this is all about
What have you got to show us that will cause us not to doubt?
What have you got that can prove your heritage?
As you claim that you are both part of her lineage
What is that document that you are waving about
Come on, show it to me so that we can work this out.

Well, who have we got here? What a sight for sore eyes
Coming face to face with you after all these years - what a
surprise

I wish I could say it was pleasant but I cannot be a hypocrite
To come in here claiming to have a right I will not permit
Where were you both when she was sick and needed you to be near?
We could do without your presence here tonight our sorrow and grief to share.

You have decided to turn up now that she has gone
You call yourselves her children, her daughter and her son?
The same way you rejected her and refused to pay her any visits
Don't bother coming around here now expecting any credit
I listened to her day and night calling out your names
She wept and cried and broke her heart in her maternal pain.

So don't come in here throwing your weight about
The way you've behaved you're no better than a lout
She needed you here to help stop her suffering
But not even a little note or a phone call were you offering
Please stop waving that piece of paper in your hand
You are not conducting an orchestra or a band.

That piece of paper as you call it
Is what's going to prove that I'm legit
What I have here is our mother's latest Will
Ha ha, that's got you hasn't it, now you've stood still
I've had this in my possession for a number of years
It will prove to you all that my sister and I are the rightful heirs.

Take that bogus piece of paper out of my face
You and your sister are a total disgrace
Instead with your mother you try to build bridges

61

You stuck with your silly pride and became very rigid
I was there on many an occasion when your mother tried to repair
relations
But you would not speak with her, you refused reconciliation.

Take your sorry self out of this house
You are nothing more than a louse
I was there and signed as one of her witnesses
When the two of you she decided to disinherit
You forced her to make a very hard decision
But your callous treatment of her forced her hand.

Go on get out of here whilst you still can
You're not welcome here you must understand
Your arrogance and your greed know no bound
If this was the Wild West, we would run you out of town
No, you cannot have a drink before you go
And the location of the funeral you will never know.

What's that you say, you're going to see a lawyer
Be my guest go and see how you will get slaughtered
If you expect anyone to be afraid of your threats
You definitely don't know who you are dealing with yet
Your mother legally registered her decision
And I for one am very glad she came to the right conclusion.

I do not recognise half you people in here
But you've not seen the last of me so don't you fear
This house belongs to us of that there is no doubt
As is all the money that is in her bank account
My sister and I will not allow you to steal our inheritance

We cared for our mother, even if we did it from a distance.

Take yourselves out of here before you get thrown out
Can't you hear the foolishness that's coming out of your mouth?
How can you look after her from afar?
You never visited though you could have travelled by bus, train or car
If you were in touch with her you would have known
That all her money was gone and even the house she no longer owns.

You mean to tell me we are poor and destitute
I don't believe you - this story I refute
My sister and I will take this further
That woman that you're robbing was our mother
Tomorrow, tomorrow we are going to get advice
Our mother worked really hard and her health she sacrificed.

Have they gone? Did you manage to get rid of them in the end
Thank you, you've turned out to be a very good friend
You all played your parts extremely well
By their words they showed no love it was easy to tell
And it broke my heart and has left me dismayed
It is a shame we had to put on this little charade
But it allowed me to see by the attitude they displayed
That their interest was not in me and I feel really betrayed.

I pondered and pondered about my decision
And now know for sure I must fulfil my mission
I now completely understand the meaning of family
It doesn't have to be blood that is just an old phantasy

Family is who treats you with love and humanity
That's why I'm giving all to friends and relatives in its totality.

My son and my daughter have revealed their true colours
They didn't care for me they just saw pound signs and dollars
As a mother it breaks my heart to see
That my children valued my possessions more than they valued
me
So come on my true friends and family let us eat drink and be
merry
I'm satisfied with the outcome though it makes me feel sad,
ashamed and sorry.
I'm happy with my decision now that I know how they will
behave when I'm gone
I'll be leaving all my worldly goods to those who will feel my loss
and will genuinely mourn.

THE DREAM

I feel as if I am living in a psychological prison
For years I have been on a personal mission
I want so badly to change my life for myself and my family
But to achieve my dream I need to have money.

I have a good voice and I know that I can sing
But convincing others is a very tricky thing
I really only just need to be given a break
But everyone I approach they want a big stake.

I want to see my name in lights
I visualise it all day and night
Just one occasion in the spotlight
I'm convinced will set me up for the rest of my life.

But my family cannot understand my passion
They think I'm on an untenable mission
I certainly do not get any encouragement from them
I do not know from where their negativity stem.

I have a determination to succeed
This is not just a dream but it has now become a need
I will continue to practice my craft
Despite the fact that some people think I'm daft.

I have just one more place to try
My excitement I am finding hard to hide
Everything depends on this audition
I must succeed, this has now become my ambition.

I turned up on time at the agreed club
The building was nothing but a run-down pub
The place was buzzing with drunken louts
And as I got on the stage I was greeted with shouts.

The noise they made was almost deafening
I was scared but was determined to remain standing
I was tempted to turn and bolt through the door
But felt I couldn't let myself down, that was for sure.

I brazened it out and started to sing
The noise was so great I didn't think they were listening
But ever so slowly the noise abated
I felt more courageous and ever so elated.

The man who had said he would be my manager
Was someone who was a complete stranger
It just goes to show how a chance meeting
Could end up being the means of you succeeding.

I bumped into the man on my way to the supermarket
My apologies he graciously acknowledged and accepted
We immediately struck up a conversation
And I told him about my lifelong plan.

So my advice to all and sundry
To stop you and your family from
going hungry
Smile and speak politely to strangers who you meet
As they could make the difference between whether you starve or
whether you eat.

Roots-

- ❖ Ode to Our Ancestors
- ❖ Self Perception
- ❖ The Lesson
- ❖ Land of My Birth
- ❖ Celebration of the Caribbean
  Social Forum (A Social Club)
- ❖ Lockdown
- ❖ Pets
- ❖ The Mother Tree
- ❖ Revenge of the Stolen Hot Food

ODE TO OUR ANCESTORS

Dear ancestors we need to let you know that after all these years
we continue to feel your pain
We are here to tell you that your sacrifice and suffering will not
have been in vain
We will never forget what you've been through and how you were
bold
Because no matter how distasteful it is, your story will be told.

The lynching and the burning seem to have happened years and
years away
But unfortunately, very similar things are still happening to us
today.
The hatred of our pigmentation seems to be systemic
It is a global phenomenon which is like an epidemic.

The hearts of the younger generation
Are heaving with pent up indignation
But we promise you we will be strong
As we try to correct the historical wrongs.

They have tried hard to write you out of history
But their motivation is no longer a mystery
And sadly, nothing much seems to have changed
We are still subjected to brutality and outrage.

We know they burnt down
Prosperous towns and businesses
And tried to sow the narrative

That you were just ignorant savages.

No longer are we prepared to sit back and internalise their lies
Because we now understand and realise
That in order for us to survive
It is necessary for us to now organise and strategies.

SELF PERCEPTION

The false perception that you have of me
Which you perpetuate for the whole world to see
Has caused me to accept, internalise and relate
So now I am filled with loathing and self-hate.

From generation to generation
And throughout many a nation
Black people have been issuing the same cry
And if we don't stop it, this will continue until we die.

How can you bring that young man here?
His skin colour doesn't even look fair
Can't you see that he's too black and ugly
Don't you see the boy resembles a monkey?

And what are you doing with that kind of girl
Her hair short and thick and look like burr burr
Can't you find a girl whose hair is tall
Is that too much to ask for after all?

And look at that one how his nose is broad
I've told you before, you cannot bring someone like this in this
yard
This one doesn't look too bad but her lips are too thick
Introducing these people to me, you are taking the mick!

I'm getting old and I need to see
Grand children and great grandchildren who look like me

I want to see that the future generations
Carry on the straight nose and light skin traditions.

Fast forward to today's young black people
They still have that same mindset and that is the trouble
The minute they introduce their new child to you
You immediately look at the skin and the hue.

What a way your baby has good hair
That will not be difficult to care
And look how her skin is clear and pretty
You must feel proud that your child is such a beautiful kiddie.

Then a little further down the street
Another friend with a baby you meet
Neither the hair nor the skin tone is to your liking
So you just look and refrain from commenting.

Back in your home you could hardly wait to get on the phone
To broadcast to the world in case they didn't know
That the child you just saw in the pram
Did not possess the same qualities as his mum.

You seem to see light skin and straight hair
As the only things worthy to declare
To become accepted as a good upstanding black person
Otherwise you continue to be a racial burden.

So young and old let us make a pact
And agree that it is no disgrace to be black
God in his wisdom fashioned us from the earth

And regardless of what others think, we are beautiful from birth.

Please open your hearts and your eyes to see
That people from all nations aspire to be
Dark and thick lipped like you and me
So stop your foolishness and make your minds free.

Join me in letting our children know
They must be proud and accept themselves as they grow
Let them know that being black is not a disgrace
But in this world a lot of prejudice they will face.

Let us stop this old illusion
That in order to get inclusion
If our complexion is nearer to the white race
Then our black ancestry will be harder to trace.

Stand up and with confidence proclaim
That given the same chances we can be the same
So our goal now for the school children is the challenge
That they will give all pupils the same knowledge.

Black children need to experience inner peace
And this should come to them with ease
If we just stop this generational self-hate
And love ourselves and each other for our mental health's sake.

THE LESSON

Gather around children let me tell you a story
It all has to do with our history
I feel I must prepare you for what you will face in this world
The reason you'll understand as the story unfolds.

You hardly hear religious stories in schools
It has become the fashion and in some places it's a rule
But the Bible tells us that thousands of years ago
God created the earth and made man, with woman in tow.

Why mankind decided to behave the way they do we don't know
But to many they have brought pure misery and woe
The first man on earth is thought to be black
But many want to dispute that this is a fact.

Hundreds of years ago in the continent of Africa
Our people roamed and didn't pay attention to the tricksters
But collaborators helped the enslavers to capture our ancestors
Who took them to what we now call the Diaspora.

They took them in their thousands to build their new world
The amount of torture and suffering
is too much to be told
They were chained and beaten and like cattle were sold
By people whose hearts were hardened and cold.

They treated their animals better than they treated their slaves
And many of our ancestors met a watery grave

As they were taken bound in ships far across the sea
Many fought desperately to remain sovereign and free.

They were thrown overboard if they got sick or rebelled
Their existence became a complete living hell
What was in their hearts we can only imagine
Because of this brutal treatment that was happening.

Our ancestors were chained and beaten and called savages
And unspeakable cruelty was inflicted under lashes
In order to try to survive and escape from the harsh punishment
Some of the slaves became docile and obedient.

When they arrived on the other side of the world
Change your name and your language they were told
But our ancestors they were brave and smart
They learnt new ways to communicate with each other, which
became an art.

Many fought for their freedom and some tried to run away
But they were tracked down with dogs and were often slain
Some were caught and brought back and had a foot cut off
As an example of the lessons that other slaves must be taught.

Freedom was never far from our ancestors' minds
And new ways of escaping they tried to find
It was very hard for them to know who to trust
But escaping to freedom for many of them, was a must.

Please don't let the history books lie to you
They tell many stories of slavery most of which were not true

Slaves were prevented from learning to read or write
As the enslavers were afraid education would strengthen their
fight.

You will hear that black people have contributed nothing to
civilisation
But let me tell you, that this is a lot of misinformation
Many gadgets have been invented by the black man
But the glory was stolen by others who had their own plans.

Because formal education was denied them
The details of many of their inventions, they were unable to pen
The white masters decided to take all the glory
And try to write black people's inventions out of history.

They also try to say it was their benevolence
That ended slavery and gave us some relevance
They conveniently forget to mention all the slave uprisings
In case further generations find it all too inspiring.

Although slavery is supposed to be abolished
I don't want you to behave in any way that could be deemed
foolish
The black man is still under subjugation, and racism is rife
And you have to be careful how you conduct your life.

Many white people will deny that they are racist
And their argument can sometimes be very persuasive
But please take it from me and don't be fooled
In many situations you could be ridiculed.

Be very careful when you are in the street
Because the racists and bigots you will surely meet
It is not always easy to recognise them
But you will know, when you see the different way they treat your
white friends.

You must also look at how you conduct yourselves
Because your actions could put many of you in police cells
There are far too many young black men dying through knife
crime
For this self destruction you must have absolutely no time.

You have a responsibility to show love and care
You should be able to walk the streets without having to fear
Please stop being one another's abuser
There are enough other races predicting that you have no future.

You cannot criticise other people's actions
Unless you are prepared to behave with compassion
Towards other people of your own race
And end these self hatred actions, which are a disgrace.

I know it is natural for you to want to have fun
But be very careful or you might end up staring down the barrel of
a gun
You cannot copy the things you see white people do
Their freedom and privilege do not include or extend to you.

I want you to read these books so that you can understand your
rights as well as your responsibilities

Because in this world you will be faced with many a fight and also great possibilities.

So now dear children I hope I've sufficiently educated you
To understand that your survival depends on the trials and tribulations you will have to go through.

LAND OF MY BIRTH

"I'm a born Jamaican" and "No matter where in the world I go I
am a Jamaican",
Are just two of the many festival songs, celebrating the wonders
of this beautiful Island.
Which many people who remain on the island, and those in the
diaspora,
Sing when they are nostalgic and want to reconnect and to
remember.

August 6th is the day when many people are acknowledging
Jamaican, as an independent nation,
And many of us believe this indeed, is a worthy cause for a great
celebration.
"Out of many one people" is the motto of the land,
And if you see the diversity of the population, it's a sentiment you
will easily understand.

Jamaica is an island in the Caribbean Sea,
It is the third largest of the islands, in the Greater Antilles.
These many years of independence is a great achievement,
But the island is not without its troubles, and woes, which have
baffled successive governments.

However, the beauty of Jamaica is something to extol,
The view from the top of the Blue Mountain, is one of many
splendours to behold.
The many splendid beaches, and the cascading waterfalls,
Are only some of the great experiences, visitors will recall.

The flora and the fauna, and the many beautiful birds,
Leaves one feeling thankful and joyful beyond words.
Jamaica's national flower is the Lignum Vitae,
And the blue mahoe is her majestic national tree.

Jamaica boasts over 200 species of the Orchid flower,
Resplendent in their various hues, and extremely vibrant colours,
And Bob Marley's One Love was danced to, at a UNESCO conference,
A feat which shows the world, Jamaica's music dominance.

His message to us, to Emancipate Ourselves from Mental Slavery,
Must be something we continue to do without any wavering.
The emotions expressed in the song Don't Worry, Because Every Little Thing Is Going to be Alright",
Serves as words of encouragement, in the face of all our troubles, and strifes.

Jamaica's national pledge. and the national anthem,
Remind us how we should live as we embrace our hard earned freedom.
"Eternal Father Bless This Land" is normally sung very lustily,
Resounding at Jamaican functions, both abroad, and also locally.

The beauty of this island further extends to the diversity of her people,
For a small island to have had four Miss World, Jamaica has shown that she is both proud and regal.
As a resilient people we continue to strive and achieve,
Beating down racial and other barriers, as for success we cleave.

The Jamaican cuisine is a definite food sensation,
That has spread far beyond our little island to many other nations.
Boston Jerk Centre and Montego Bay Jerk Pit,
Are two great eating places which to visitors and locals alike, are
most definitely hits.

The roast yam and salt fish, jerk pork and jerk chicken,
Are all so very delicious, they are truly finger licking.
Curry goat, roast Breadfruit, fried dumpling with ackee and salt
fish, or maybe callaloo,
Are just a few of the many exquisitely tasty Jamaican dishes you
will continually flock to.

Guinness punch, John crow batty, and Jamaican white rum,
Are some of the local drinks which could help you to have a little
more fun.
Snow cone, fudge, shave ice, and Devon house ice cream,
Are other great delights to accompany the Jamaican cuisine.

"We lickle but we talawa" meaning we are small but we are great,
Is a sentiment which is true and definitely no mistake.
Shelly-Ann Fraser Pryce and Usain Bolt, demonstrate that with
their sprint,
Which they execute with grace, and speed, before you or I can
even blink.

Thinking of Jamaican heroes including Nanny, and her brother
Cojoe,
Make us realise that as a nation we still have a long way to go.

Their fighting spirit to free Jamaica from slavery, and British dominance,
Has sadly in some instances today, seem almost like an irrelevance.

My message to you my dear fellow Jamaicans, and friends of Jamaica,
Is that we can all think of our various island homes with a great sense of nostalgia.
But let us come together and ask for peace, and God's grace and favour,
To continuously bless the island of Jamaica, and propel her into the world, as a positive trail blazer.

Many people of prominence have hailed from this little island,
Where the residents constantly smile at you and tell you "no problem".
So let us all pray to the Lord above,
To richly bless Jamaica, Land we love!

CELEBRATION OF CARIBBEAN SOCIAL FORUM (A SOCIAL CLUB)

Lockdown and not shutdown has been the mantra for the past year
We have been subjected to being restricted because of the pandemic fear
But the brave attendees of the Caribbean Social Forum
All decided to tune in and continue to act with dignity and decorum.

We have not stinted on any entertainment
Many things have been put in place for our merriment
We've had lectures on food and feet
And we've even had our own discussion about our teeth.

People have been exercising their vocal chords
Some singing out of tune because of the lack of a keyboard.
But it looked like a good time was had by all who participated
Even if some of them sounded as if they were being castrated!

Celebrating is what the Caribbean Social Forum does best
If you don't believe me, let us put it to the test
Barbados, St Vincent and the Grenadiers, Trinidad and Jamaica have all had their share
Of celebrating their independence through history, quizzes and such other things, at the appropriate times of the year.

Religious discussions and weekly quizzes
Help us to face challenges as well as testing our knowledge

But the main function of the Caribbean Social Forum
Is to help us keep connected, having a laugh and having fun.

Fifty-two weeks we have been on zoom
Connecting with each other in our own front rooms
It has not been an easy time for some
Because sickness, sorrow and losses have been the outcome.
But the love and support that the members generate
Is heart-warming and helps to ease the heartaches.

Six years of brightening people's lives
Has been something that helps many of us to survive
Tuning in from all different parts of the globe
Some dressed up in their Sunday best whilst others were zooming
in their bathrobes
But the fact that to participate, they were driven
Is testimony to the importance that the Forum is given.

The last year could have been long, difficult and lonely
But we have been able to stay connected, all be it remotely
People have evidenced their true commitment
Their presence on the platform makes that very evident.

So to members of the Caribbean Social Forum both old and new
ones
Let us thank the Founder of this incredible social club for all the
hard work she has done
Also give yourselves a clap for what you've achieved
By celebrating six years of holding each other up, through a
support system which is successful beyond belief.

LOCKDOWN

Lockdown not shut down, is the Caribbean Social Forum's mantra
But gone are the days of hugs and the incessant chatter
No more banging or clatter of dominoes
No more slight looks which are the secret codes.

Lockdown not shut down, is something we have come to accept
All these life changes, we have to learn to respect
No more scrabble, and looking for a play out
We have to develop other interests as our daily lives we have to
go about.

Lockdown not shut down, has been a very hard lesson for some
But this is now the new reality of what life has become
No more bingo, no more scrabble or any other games
We have to be careful that all our days don't become the same.

Lockdown not shut down, is a good chance for many
New hobbies and interests have flourished a plenty
No more whispering to your neighbour
No more asking for that little favour.

Lockdown not shutdown, has also been very cruel
For some people intense loneliness, it has fuelled
No reason to get up, get dressed and come out;
Shut away in doors, doing your best not to scream and shout.

Lockdown not shut down, has brought with it some heavy blows
Wreaking much pain and suffering in its throws

Lives of great men remind us all our lives can be sublime
But all humans are great, when they leave their footprints on the
sand of time.

During this lockdown we have lost a few soldiers
Their simple act of kindness has supported us like bolsters
That smile, that touch, those words of encouragement
Will not be shut down as they will always be remembered, with
gratitude and reverence.

Lockdown not shut down has caused many of us to grieve in
silence
When our loved ones have departed and we desperately miss their
presence
As a community we are used to personally showing our support
But with this situation we have to depend on reports.

Lockdown not shut down, is a wonderful concept
It helps us to remember who we were from the outset
The losses many of us have experienced of late
Have helped us to reflect and renew our faiths.

Our loved ones have gone before us and sometimes we don't
understand why
But God's plans were made, and we all have to die
They've gone before us to prepare our place
And as painful as it is, we have to accept it with grace.

Well intentioned words of sorrow do not compensate
For the tremendous empty feeling that seems to be our fate

But having people who understand and know what we're going through
Is helpful in making us focus on what we have to do.

May the souls of our dear departed, rest in eternal peace
The knowledge that their suffering is over, will help us to believe
That they've gone to a better place which is full of light and love
They will be still with us, and protecting us from above.

So sincere condolences are being sent your way
May you find peace and comfort, in the simple things we say
Please be assured that your loved ones will always be remembered
And their lives and accomplishments will always be honoured.

So, as we continue to grieve and to remember
It is not easy when we see the empty chair, or the empty place on the sofa
But the special memories in the love we had found
Makes it easier to accept these things whilst we're in lockdown, but are not shut down!

PETS

I had a conversation with a friend in the Caribbean
Telling her about things she could never imagine
The way these people in this country
Treat animals of all types and variety.

I told her that people make pets out of gerbils
I can tell you, she was far from thrilled
When I explained that they looked just like rats
She accused me of not talking facts.

I told her the gerbils were in the house in a cage
Fed, and had a wheel on which all day they spun
She wanted to know what the attraction was
And I told her people watched them, and for them this was fun.

I then told her about the rabbits
She was puzzled, and said she didn't get it
I explained they were kept in a hutch
And she wanted to know why they were taken from the bush.

I told her that for some people rabbit was meat
She thought this was acceptable and could be quite a treat
But when I told her that rabbits were also kept as pets
Her look of astonishment I'll never forget.

I was now really fired up, as I told her about the birds
My narrative seemed to have left her short of words
Especially those that were not in a cage in the house

But those who were free and flying about
I explained that they were fed from bird houses which were
sometimes crude
And it wasn't just stale bread or unwanted food
But some people actively went out and bought bird seeds
To them, to feed wild birds were rewarding deeds.

I then told her about the cats
She was scandalised when she heard that
Cats were not kept in the house to catch rats
They were companions with whom adults and children interact.

Her sense of disbelief I could not avert
As she expressed her horror when she learnt
That cats had beds and litter trays in their special space
I really had to convince her that that really was the case
They were often in people's laps when not on their beds
She said she couldn't believe, she really heard what I had said.

It was the treatment of the dogs which, however left her
speechless
She couldn't believe animals were treated with so much love and
respect
I told her that during winter months dogs were dressed in coats
She told me to hold on, as she just had to take notes.
I explained that their owners, didn't want them to feel the cold
And that they drank their water and ate their food from their own
special doggie bowls
They are bought food and are fed special diets
She laughed so loud, I had to persuade her to be quiet!

I explained that some little dogs, who can be ever so cute
Are treated like babies and are sometimes put in prams, in which
they commute
They are also carried in their owner's arms
That news really filled her with great alarm.

She couldn't believe people made it a daily ritual
To take their dogs for their daily walks, which became habitual
When I said some dogs slept in their owner's beds
She said that was nasty, the dogs should sleep in the shed.

The part of the story that really appalled her
And what she found really bizarre
Is the fact that when the dogs poo on the street or in the park,
The owners have to clean it up as they walk
She ended by saying foreigners are strange
Because they behave as if they're deranged
It seems as if the animals are revered
More than humans are, to her, it would appear.

When I told her that some dog owners allow their pet to lick their
face
She told me to keep quiet, as that was a disgrace
I laughed and told her she hadn't heard the best
And she said there just couldn't be anything more that her
imagination could test
I told some owners kiss their pets on the lips
And that bit over information, really made her flip.

I told her she hadn't heard anything yet
As I explained that when pets are sick, they get taken to the vet

At this point she really thought that I was joking
And laughed so much, that she ended up choking.

I definitely left the best for last
And told her what happens to most pets when they depart
She said that it sounded really scary
To hear that pets get buried in their own pet cemeteries
So, her great wish when she departs this world,
Is to comes back as a pet in one of these crazy foreigner's
household.

THE MOTHER TREE

Where are you going? I asked the little boy as he raced down the
garden path
I'm going to look at the Mother Tree
He shouted back at me
The Mother Tree? What on earth is a Mother Tree?
As he ran along, he said, just follow me and you will see.

We reached a clearing at the edge of some woods
Where a huge magnificent oak tree stood
This is the Mother Tree the boy gushed
Isn't it great? He said in a voice that was hushed.

I had to admit it was a beautiful tree
Majestic and strong as its branches waved in the breeze
Yes, it is a beautiful tree, I said
As I carefully looked where I tread.

But why do you call it a Mother Tree?
He looked almost angry as he shouted back at me
Grown-ups are so silly; I don't understand why they cannot see
So please listen while I tell you how this tree allows me to be.

The tree has many branches to keep me safe and sound
I always feel protected by my Mother Tree when I'm around
If I'm in the garden and it starts to rain
I know what I can do to relieve any strain.

I run up to the Mother Tree and get under a branch
It shelters me and keeps me dry, and gives me another chance
To run about and play to my heart's content
Without having to go inside because I am drenched.

If the sun is too hot and I need to cool down
I get under my tree where I sit and listen to the sounds
Its branches act like umbrellas, that shelter me from the heat
I feel happy and relaxed, it really is a treat.

The branches sway gracefully, keeping me nice and cool
I then imagine that I'm in an air-conditioned room, or in a
swimming pool.

If I am feeling lonely, or if I want to cry
I run to my Mother Tree, fling my arms around its trunk, knowing
that I have an ally
I swear that the branches bow down
And the leaves stroke my furrowed brow.

When I have a secret that I know I cannot tell
I whisper it to the Mother Tree because I know it will keep my
secret well.

I was impressed by this little boy as he spoke about his Mother
Tree
And I thanked him most sincerely, for explaining it to me.
With a mischievous smile and a giggle, he asked
Do you want to know the best part?
I nodded my head in answer
Which made the little boy almost collapse with laughter.

When I'm in the garden, if ever I'm caught short
I don't bother to go into the house, I just take a brisk walk
I hurry to my Mother Tree
Pull my pants down, and just let out my wee.

I was appalled by what I heard and he must have seen it in my
face
Because he quickly reassured me, that this was no disgrace.
My Mother Tree is full of love, and grace and acceptance
It doesn't matter what I do, it offers no resistance.

And also, please remember
That not everyone has someone significant they want to honour
So lady, I hope you understand that for people like me without a
loving mother
The thing that has guided and sheltered me
Has been my strong and beautiful Mother Tree.

REVENGE OF THE STOLEN HOT FOOD

I didn't really mean to steal, I had no need to, but I was greedy
I watched my mother in the kitchen and counted every dumpling
dropped in the pot, rather wearily
I knew I couldn't wait for dinner time
The thought of the dumpling, helped me to make up my mind.

Corn dumplings were my favourite and I was impatient for my
food
I dipped a spoon into the pot, found the biggest dumpling, which
put me in a very fine mood
I forgot to get some paper, and the dumpling was very hot
I couldn't think where to put it, I really was in a spot!

As I turned with the dumpling in the spoon
I heard footsteps, I panicked as I felt someone would be here soon
Someone was coming, they were approaching the kitchen
Oh, my goodness, I could not afford to get caught, not whilst I
was on this mission.

I looked around frantically for somewhere to hide the dumpling
If I got caught, that would be really something
I know how they like to give people nickname
And to be called "dumpling thief" would have been such a shame.

Oh, why didn't I just turn around and throw the dumpling back
into the pot?
No one would have known, so I wouldn't have got attacked
But my greed overruled common sense

That's the only excuse I can think of in my defence.

I looked wildly around the kitchen
As the footsteps were steadily approaching
I was getting more and more frantic, As I slipped the hot
dumpling in my trouser pocket.

What a huge mistake I had made
As my leg was seared with unexpected pain
I began to hop about, and it was all I could do not to shout out
loud.
The kitchen door opened and I started to dance
The pain only shifted as I pranced and pranced.

I'm still not sure who was standing in front of me
I was blinded by unshed tears, and I couldn't see
I made up my mind that I had to run, in the hope that the hot
dumpling would cool down.

But the dumpling seemed to have had a mind of its own
And continued to burn me without any mercy
I can still feel the pain, as I look at the scar which I couldn't
explain
And remember the lesson I was taught that day
If you think you're going to get caught stealing dumpling out of
the pot
Don't be foolish enough to put it in your pocket, especially when
you could have put it in your hat!

But did I learn my lesson, it's really hard to tell
Especially when the chocolate tea had such an inviting smell

I only intended to take a taste but it was so good I grabbed a cup
I knew I shouldn't have taken so much.

I could taste the nutmeg and the cinnamon, as I leisurely sipped
the hot delicious drink
I was transported with each mouthful, and didn't even think
Getting caught had not entered my thought
I knew if anyone found out, I would have been distraught.

But as I became aware of someone approaching
I knew I had to do something, I could not take the reproaching
I had no choice but to toss the remaining drink into my mouth
I don't k now which hurt the most
My sore tongue or my scorched throat.

As I got older my food stealing got bolder
But I eventually had to stop, I was becoming reckless
Before my entire body betrayed my weakness
The hot soup was such a disaster
It scorched places where I couldn't put a plaster.

But my hot food exploits came to an end last Sunday
When I decided to try the rice and peas, before dinner
It was almost as if I was being spied upon, as I raised the spoon to
my mouth
I had no time to chew, otherwise I would have been found out
Have you ever swallowed hot rice? if you haven't, please don't try
it
Stealing hot food, is such an awful risk
The rice missed my tongue, it missed my throat, and burnt me in
my stomach!

Hot peas soup has also been part of my loot
But now I don't steal food unless it is cool
So please take heed and pay attention to this message
The worse of all is stealing hot cornmeal porridge
All hot food has its own way of making sure you don't succeed
It burns you in all different places, and takes revenge against your greed!

Not Indoors –

- ❖ The Walk
- ❖ Care of self and Others
- ❖ My Peace
- ❖ Allure of the Puddle
- ❖ Self Destruction
- ❖ Youth Exuberance
- ❖ Gratitude

THE WALK

I took a stroll up to the park today
And I met an elderly gentleman on the way
I wondered if he would acknowledge me or say hello
But as we passed each other he smiled, raised a hand and said
"mind how you go".

The encounter though very brief
Left me feeling mellow and relieved
Until that moment I had not fully realised my loneliness
And I felt that the raised hand, the sound of his voice and the
smiling eyes were not just politeness.

I continued my walk with renewed energy
I vowed to commit this to memory
My walk through the park was so different
Everything took on such a new essence.

The birds that flitted about sang sweeter
The flowers and grass seemed neater
The leaves on the trees appeared green and bright
All in all, everything appeared to radiate much more, light.

As other people on my walk I passed
I vowed to give them more than a cursory glance
I might even pluck up the courage to smile
As that was something, I knew I hadn't done for a while.

I really don't know now what is considered to be normal
I don't want to appear either too over friendly nor indeed not too
formal
I have lived on my own for so long
I just don't want to do anything wrong.

It took a lot of courage for me to leave my house
I have been a recluse for many months
But the walls had started to close in on me
Which made me decide to get out and see how I feel.

That gentleman was the first person I met on my walk
I wondered what I would have done if he had decided to talk
But the kindness and understanding I detected in his smile
Almost brought tears of gratitude to my eyes.

Today I decided was an experiment
Going out and meeting others was my intent
How I would have been perceived I did not know
But the first person I met told me to watch how I go.

I definitely will try this again next week
Because human connection and friendship is what I seek
Or maybe I might even risk going out tomorrow
It might help to stem my loneliness and sorrow.

I went to bed in a sombre mood
My mind was so churned up I didn't even want food
Do I dare go out for another walk so soon?
Maybe it would be better not to go in the morning but to go in the
afternoon.

In the morning I got up and dressed very carefully
I felt it was important how I looked and I set out hopefully
The afternoon sun was shining ever so brightly
As I walked in a manner which I hoped was jauntily.

I followed the same route I had taken the day before
In my heart I was hoping to meet the same people but I didn't
want to appear a bore
As I walked towards the park with a heart full of hope
I craved meaningful relationships with which I could cope.

The first person I met was an elderly lady
What struck me most was her obvious frailty
We passed each other without a word
And I began to think that was too absurd.

Already I'd forgotten my earlier intention
To make some friends had been my mission
I did not want to go back to that cold unfriendly house
To live there alone and be as quiet as a mouse.

I made a silent vow that the next person I meet
Even if they don't, I certainly would speak
I continued resolutely on my way
Rehearsing in my mind what I would say.

Oh heavens, my heart skipped a beat
And I stood rooted to the spot as if I had clay feet
Because right there in my line of vision
Came the real reason for this excursion.

"Mind how you go", he smilingly said
And all the blood rushes to my head
"The same to you" I shyly utter
And was embarrassed that my voice came out in a stutter.

He stopped in his tracks and started walking back
And I stood there in complete and utter shock
As he asked "do you come walking everyday"
I got tongue tied and didn't know what to say.

Do I lie and say yes or do I tell him the truth?
I was battling with my conscience and stood there mute
He stood there looking at me quizzically
And I decided I must answer him honestly.

Before I knew it, I was telling him the story of my life
I related all my woes, all my battles and all my strife
To this complete stranger I bared my soul
And marvelled at myself how I could have been so bold.

I began to feel embarrassed and foolish
And waited for a response which I suspected would be brutish
But he gave me the most beautiful and wonderful smile
As he slowly held out his hand and took mine.

He congratulated me for being so bold
As his own interesting life story, he told
His own life was also one big mess
He too was living with a lot of anxiety and stress.

The joy that rushed in my heart I can never explain
I thanked the gods that the decision I had made was not made in vain
My quest for friendship had paid dividends
As I realised that this gentleman and I would become firm friends.

CARE FOR SELF AND OTHERS

Do we consider ourselves more valuable than anyone else?
This is a question we must continually ask ourselves
Are we incapable of understanding the needs of others?
Is it necessary that we must always be told and reminded that we
could all potentially suffer?

There is a protocol on how we should behave
In order our own lives and the lives of others we could save
But some people seem to have no understanding
So the rules they are continuously flouting or bending.

Walking in a group of four or five is not acceptable
Because the walkway is for everyone and should be accessible
Sociologists tell us about the selfish gene
But it is hard to believe in its existence, unless it is seen.

The human species are very diverse
Fortunately, we are not the only life on earth
I often wonder if the same behaviour exists in the animal kingdom
Or if animals conduct their lives with a lot more wisdom.

When you're walking or standing two or three abreast
Please have some consideration for the rest of us
We should not have to ask you to move out of the way
That action should be taken automatically, without any sway.

To everyone their own life is precious
Although some people's action seems positively malicious

I do not know if it is because they do not understand
Why they behave as if it is inconsequential if their numbers
expand.

No one is saying you cannot meet and talk
But please give the rest of us some space to walk
Just remaining standing and looking at us as we advance
Is not helpful, it is rather an inappropriate stance.

Spending time socialising and making connections
Is a natural human need and ambition
But we must show some consideration
And behave towards others with love and compassion.

Everyone is doing their best to survive
By doing all they can to keep themselves alive
So please show some understanding and do your part
Giving way, will only fractionally disrupt your talk.

How long are we expected to let you selfish people dictate
And be responsible for the outcome of our destiny and the balance
of our fate?
From today I feel it is necessary that we take a stand that will
affect all our futures
By asking you politely to practice walking in single files and
desist from being groupers.

Take a look at all of God's creations
All around the entire world and in every nation
Please remember that our survival depends on our actions
And the necessity to treat each other with more consideration.

At first you might find it hard to break the habit
You like to walk together- I understand, truly I get it
But the world belongs to all of us and we must learn to share
So, when you're out remember your responsibility not only to
others, but also to yourself for your own self-care.

MY PEACE

I decided to sit out in my garden and do some reflection
It was necessary to free my mind from a certain situation.
The sun was shining oh so brightly
That I felt compelled to say thanks to the Almighty.

I quietly gazed at the leaves on the trees
And watched as they gently swayed in the breeze.
My gaze took me further and further afield
And I looked in wonder at what was revealed.

Through the trees and the leaves, the blue sky was peeping
The magnificence of the view through my heart was seeping.
I sat and pondered at God's creation
And I was filled with tremendous joy and elation.

I decided to take a careful look around the garden
To see what else could ease my mind of its burden.
I saw beautiful butterflies flittering around
They seemed to be in a hurry although they didn't make a sound.

There was a bird nest way high in a tree
And birds flying in and out was all I could see.
If there were eggs or chicks in that nest
I had no idea; I would just have to take a guess.

Somewhere behind me something was buzzing
It definitely was not a bee because it would have been humming.
I looked around quickly and saw a great big fly

Which pitched on my arm as it flew carelessly by.

But alas my reflective silence did not last
As I sat and watched nature rushing pass.
The neighbour's children were out and about
And as you will appreciate little people tend to cry and shout.

The noise was getting to be really very distracting
As all my sense of peace and tranquillity they were attacking.
I wondered if I should get up and go inside
Because all this loud noise I just couldn't abide.

I sat outside for a little while longer
As the noise from across the fence got stronger.
Then through the noise and crying I heard a little girl sing
And that made me think of the peace and joy, singing can bring.

Because it is impossible to shut out all that's around
I made a decision to embrace and enjoy every sound.
Although my tranquillity and silence were broken
It was reassuring that my senses were stimulated and woken.

THE ALLURE OF THE PUDDLE

I am always fascinated when I go to the park
To see the different activities as I take my daily walk
Dogs of all description straining at the leash
Whilst others walk sedately or run at their owners' heels.

Football players, marking out their pitch
Weighing up their chances, before deciding on that kick
Joggers running past me, many dripping with sweat
Not even remembering how many laps they've done, but hey,
what the heck!

Men, women, boys and girls
On bicycles, or skates, doing their daily twirls
Little children on tricycles, encouraged by their parents
Should they take a tumble, there is seldom any lament.

But the thing I find most intriguing
The thing that has me quickly breathing
Are the shapes I can clearly see in the puddles
They are all so very different, there's no chance of getting into a
muddle.

Most look like maps of different countries of the world
You don't have to use much imagination, as the images unfurl
As you gaze at the contours, and recognise the place
You congratulate yourself, and the joy can be seen in your face.

Puddles can be seen at different places in the park
Not just on the concrete, but even on the grass
Some are very clear, whilst others are muddy
But the children think they're glorious, as they splash about in their wellies!

SELF DESTRUCTION

I have a message for today's black youths
Sit down, and keep quiet, whilst I tell you some home truths
You are becoming a racial embarrassment
And it is important that your behaviour, you amend.

You are the descendants of a proud race of people
Who have endured unspeakable hardships through spurious
reasons
History has documented black people's struggles and sufferings
You must be aware of it, that's why your actions are so puzzling.

Do you look at yourself before you leave your home?
Your appearance alone makes you look as if you're suffering from
some rare syndrome
Wearing your trousers hanging down under your bottom that way
Is not a fashion statement, it's an idiotic movement which makes
you a definite prey.

You need to start conducting your life with pride
Because your racial identity you cannot hide
Your actions do not only affect you
They impact negatively on many others too.

I'm not pretending that times are not tough
Many of you feel that you've suffered enough
But take a good look in the history books
And you will see that if you carry on like this, all black youths
will be labelled as hoodlums and crooks.

Walking around with your underpants exposed
Will not mean you will go about unopposed
Young men you need to take pride in yourselves
Instead of going around as if you cannot afford to buy belts.

This negative behaviour has gone way too far, and needs to be
curbed
It only makes you look both stupid and absurd
Learn to think positively and stop behaving so negatively
Joining gangs and hanging out with bad people will not give you
status or popularity.

Life is short enough without you making it shorter
It is imperative that you stop all this slaughter
Instead of harming others who look like you
Think instead of any good things you can do
To turn your lives around and become good role models
Be the bigger person and help to end the senseless squabbles.

They say America's yesterday, is Britain's tomorrow
And you need to look at what is happening to black men there
with sorrow
Many of them live their lives on the edge
It is therefore no wonder so many of them end up dead.

I do not know what more to say to you
As you don't seem to understand the damage you do
When your grandparents were young, they had to fight racists in
the national front

There were thugs with chains and baseball bats who they had to confront
But the lesson that you should take from your elders about that time
Is that they supported each other in fighting their common enemy, not fighting each other as that to them, would have been seen as a crime.

Bob Marley tells us to emancipate ourselves from mental slavery
I know that because of your issues that will require a lot of bravery
However, he went on to say none but yourself can free your minds
So, reflect and you will see that there's a great message in those two lines.
Low self-image and self-loathing are destroying the black race
And this is the reality we all have to face.

Now let us look at the level of crimes involving knives
It's as if you have no incentive to value your own lives
Carrying a knife does not make you a person to be admired
Instead, it makes you more of a target or someone with whom the devil has conspired.

Don't you get tired of seeing mothers crying?
Can't you acknowledge how hard your parents have been trying?
Being poor is no excuse for killing one another so senselessly
Why are you all so bent on treating each other with so much brutality?

Young people please put down your weapons
Go back to school and get an education

You are the future of the black race
And as such, many obstacles you will have to face
Our ancestors have already paved the way by sacrificing their
lives
To give us hope and to make sure that we survive
So please show others who look like you some love and
compassion
Let peace and understanding become the new fashion.

Young people please watch the way you behave
I really do not understand why you always seem to be in such a
rage
Our future as a race looks very bleak
So, your cooperation your brothers and sisters now desperately
seek.

Your elders and definitely your ancestors are appealing to you
To turn your lives around and start thinking anew
You need to get serious and change your actions
Otherwise, you're heading for complete self destruction
We are so tired of seeing our children in either their coffins or in
handcuffs
Come on young people, by now even you must realise, that things
have gone way too far, and that enough is enough!!

YOUTHFUL EXUBERANCE

I was very surprised to see so many young people in the park
They seemed to be playing about and having a lark
My impression was that they were being irresponsible
The grass was wet, muddy and looked really miserable.

When we see a group of young people together
We seldom think that they are there to create something to treasure
Some people immediately jump to the conclusion
That these youngsters are in collusion to create havoc and destruction.

The fact that we might be wrong never gets mentioned
These young people are never asked about their intention
It has become too easy to demonise all people who are young
For the misdeeds the minority of their peers have done.

As I almost completed my first lap
I came across a spectacle which made me stop
I was so cross with myself afterwards
Because I didn't think to take a photograph.

When I was on my second round
I saw something which made me frown
I again saw a second group of youngsters
They were having the time of their lives, and they were definitely not behaving like gangsters.

I was aware of a lot of noise and shouting
And I took the time to listen to what they were mouthing
They appeared to have been encouraging one another
Amidst a lot of good humoured banter and laughter.

I decided to draw near and take a closer look
And what I saw got me definitely hooked
These young people were being very creative
They were demonstrating that youngsters can show their initiative.

A very thin sprinkling of snow had fallen on the ground
Which it seemed impossible to turn into anything profound
But they used their hands and implements to gather up the little bit
of snow
And they all got involved in patting and shaping the image that
they wanted to show.

I had to go back and review my first impression
I did not see that these young people had such a clear vision
To create something which was truly beautiful to see
And if you had witnessed it, I think you would have readily
agreed.

Out of that little scrap of snow they managed to create something
spectacular
Which I feel sure with walkers, will be immensely popular
I learnt a very valuable lesson today
And that's not to judge before knowing what I can factually say.

Some young people are never given a chance
Many of them are dismissed at a glance

So often they are seen and described as feckless
A phrase which is both discouraging and reckless.

I would urge the general public not to be so judgemental
But to realise that young people have a whole lot of potential
To demonstrate the many positive things, they are capable of
And for most, if not all of us, that knowledge should be enough.

Some older people need to understand
That the world belongs to the younger generation
They are definitely able to create things of beauty
By showcasing their diverse skills through breath-taking artistry.

So for some people who doubt the talents of the youths
Stick around long enough to explore the truth
At times when we think they are being mischievous, disruptive or
revolutionary
They are just showing us that they are talented, creative and
visionary.

GRATITUDE

Look over there, look, look, look at the sun
Look, look where I'm pointing, be quick before it goes down
Where, where should I look, I cannot see a thing
Are you sure all of this is not your imaginings?

Look, look there between the two houses
Hurry up, because the cloud might hide it, go on put on your
glasses
Oh yes, I see it, but why do you think it is so special?
Being able to see is not a coincidence, it is not something that's
incidental.
Thank you, God, for the gift of sight
To appreciate the sun, and its brilliant light.

Now look over there, look beyond the trees
The golden sunset as it reflects on the leaves
Look, can't you see what I'm showing you?
Look at the sky above, it is so blue
There it is, follow the line of my hand, and behold
The beautiful sunset is something to extoll
Thank you, Lord, that I can raise my hand
To be able to point, so that my friend could see and understand.

Look at those leaves, as they fall from the trees
It appears they have formed a pattern, for us all to see
The various colours of orange, green and brown
Look like a tapestry, arranged on the ground
Yes, I can see exactly what you mean

It is indeed, a magnificent scene
Thank you, God, for an open mind
That has helped me to appreciate this beautiful find.

Oh, my goodness, just look at that tree
It looks like someone has done that deliberately
What, are you telling me you cannot see the shape?
The tree is completely leafless, and that cannot be a mistake
If I was an artist, and knew how to sketch
This would be one of the first things, I would etch
Oh yes, I can see now what you mean
This is the first bald tree I have ever seen
Thank you, God, for allowing me to be observant
And to appreciate these wonders without any deferment.

Listen, to that, just listen to the sounds
Nature is assaulting us, all around
The different pitches in the birds' songs
Makes it easy to distinguish each one
I cannot tell one sound from another
All it means is that some birdsongs are louder
Come on let us stand quietly for a while
Listen very keenly, the songs are different in their styles
Oh yes, I can hear it now, oh this is perfect
You are right about the songs, what you said was correct
Thank you, God, for allowing me to hear
It is wonderful to realise that my hearing is clear.

Look at the squirrel as it scuttles up that tree trunk
It's turning around to look at us, before it does a bunk
Look at its bushy tail, and its wide frightened eyes

It seems as if it's afraid of us, but I fear that's just it's guile
And look at those white birds on the green grass
The two different colours, are such a lovely contrast
Look up at those birds, flying in unison
They appear to be going on a very special mission
Thank you, God, that I can walk
That I can see, and that I can talk
Thank you, God, for my appreciative attitude
Please accept my thanks and my undying gratitude.

And Much More -

- ❖ The Accident
- ❖ Grandparents Special Gift
- ❖ A Baby
- ❖ Advice to Teenagers
- ❖ The Lies
- ❖ Social Distancing
- ❖ Unfounded Fear
- ❖ The Gift

THE ACCIDENT

I took a leisurely stroll down the road feeling serene and content
Because giving my friend a big surprise was my mission and
intent
As I sauntered along my attention was drawn
To the constant blaring of the car horns.

The busses and the lorries were rushing by
I had to catch that bus, I really needed to try
Add the ringing of the bicycle bells to the mix
I realised trying to cross the road at that point would be a great
risk.

I hurried down to the zebra crossing
Someone bumped into me as they were passing
Not a word of apology did they utter
I was annoyed but, in the end, decided it really didn't matter.

I was halfway across the road when I heard the commotion
Exactly what was going on I had no notion
I was hell bent on catching that bus
So had no time to find out because I was in a rush.

I still had quite a long way to go
But the pavement was thick with people moving to and fro
I had no idea why there were so many people about
I was distracted when I heard somebody say, "watch out".

I looked back and my eyes locked with that of a man whose face
was full of fury
I wasn't sure if his anger was directed at someone else or at me
But from the look on his face, I didn't bother to enquire
I really didn't want to experience the full force of his anger.

My steps were now measured as I tried to walk more carefully
I didn't want to bump into anyone else accidentally
But my bus in the distance I could see clearly
And it's imperative I catch it, but fighting through the crowd was
making me tired and weary.

At long last I could see I was near the bus stop
But when I eventually reached, my face dropped
I couldn't believe the notice which I read there
I felt sick to my stomach and my heart filled with fear.

Not one bus was stopping in this area today
The notice filled me with utter dismay
I felt that I'd already walked several miles
And the weariness and frustration within me began to rise.

What was I to do now, I began to wonder
I stood stock still and began to ponder
Should I try to carry on or go back home
And give her a surprise call on the phone?

I figured I had come too far to give up now
I had to find my way to her house somehow
I stood there and tried to formulate a plan
I wished I was a fairy who could just wave a magic wand.

Now I understood why there were so many people about
They were going in all directions, east west north and south
There seemed to be a lot of confusion as people made their way
But where they were all going I could neither guess nor say.

I had no idea how long I had been walking
But the journey wasn't too bad because I met some people with
whom I was talking
Everyone was thinking and wondering the same
Not knowing exactly who or what was to blame.

Walking was good exercise I consoled myself
It is something positive that would enhance my health
But gosh, I am tired and ever so hungry
And the weather wasn't good as it started to get muggy.

Thank goodness, I could see her road straight ahead
There was a shop on the corner and I stopped and bought some
cheese and a loaf of bread
I could contribute that to the food I knew she would have in her
house
Had I done the right thing? I was beginning to have my doubts.

At last, I was standing outside her door
I knocked and knocked until my knuckles were almost sore
Was she in the garden or had she gone further?
I redoubled my efforts and knocked even firmer.

I listened but could not even hear a rustle inside

I began to feel anxious as I waited and waited and wondered why
she had not replied
My friend was a private person but I decided to check with the
neighbour
I didn't hesitate because anyway, I was in need of a favour.

I knocked on the neighbour's door with a sense of great urgency
I was beginning to feel panicked as this was becoming an
emergency
Why don't someone come and answer the door
I was out a long time and didn't think I could take much more.

I began to get desperate and started to march up and down
The neighbour eventually opened the door with a ferocious frown
It was a good thing that my accident was only a pee
It would have been so much more embarrassing if I was bursting
to do a dee!

GRANDPARENTS' PRECIOUS GIFT

Whenever a new baby is born into a family
It is something that grandparents greet most happily
They are blessed with the most precious gift
A gift that has helped their hearts to soar with the most glorious
lift
Especially in this time of depression, loss and
isolation
It is even more fantastic that they've been given this wonderful
distraction.

Many grand parents have joined the club of the elite
There are many of them, though each one is unique
Amongst all the overwhelming challenges
With a grandchild, grandparents have been given another chance
to have new and exciting experiences.

When a little baby girl or a baby boy is born
Whether late at night or in the early hours of the morn
There is love and excitement abounding
For grandparents, this fantastic feeling can sometimes seem
almost overwhelming.

Another little soul for family and friends to treasure
But the elation of the grandparents is more than can be measured
Their tasks as enforcers of discipline and givers of extra hugs and
kisses
Are roles they will relish, as well as granting many of their
grandchildren's wishes.

Children are sent to us as a blessing
Although their needs and demands can at times be pressing
But what a marvellous time to rejoice
As the little miracles help us to forget, what and who we have lost.

So my congratulations to all the very proud parents
Who have a responsibility which will be intense
But I hope that as they embark on this very important journey
They will remember and include the very proud grandpas and grannies!

A BABY

What is a baby except a bundle of joy?
A beautiful helpless soul, who must be cherished, and not be treated as a toy.

What is a baby except a ray of hope?
Who despite their many demands, adults somehow manage to cope.

What is a baby except a light for a bright future?
An innocent little person who looks to their parents and others to be their teachers.

What is a baby but a heart stopper?
Who grabs your finger and gurgles, and cause adults to turn foolish, incoherent and sometimes even stutter!

When a child is born, they stretch you to your limit
A baby redeems faith, lightens the heart, and lifts the spirit.

A baby is not just sleepless nights, dirty nappies and smelly bum
The sight of a new born baby can cause the most talkative person to become dumb.

The parents of a new born baby are charged with a lot of responsibility
They quickly learn that a baby needs to be nurtured, protected, and loved unconditionally.

What is a baby except an expression of love?
A mystery and a complex bundle, who spends a lot of time
gurgling and cooing like a dove.

A baby brings out the passion in their parents and many others
Who have to make sure they behave in a way that the baby's
personality is not smothered.

Babies need to be allowed to thrive and grow
They must not be spoilt, though that is a tall order, I know.

Babies sense the difference between right and wrong
They know when the love for them is either lukewarm or strong.

And as the baby grows and takes on their own personality
Parents and grandparents, uncles, aunts and cousins
Lament at what they think they are missing.

Children are a gift given to their parents for a while
They will make their parents, sigh and sometimes cry but mostly
they will make them smile.

Babies come through their parents but they have their own minds
And it is up to the adults in their lives, to help them to succeed and
shine.

What does a baby need to thrive?
Except the fierce love that gives their parents that drive.
That feeling that they will do anything to keep their child safe
No matter how much hard work, or heartache it takes.

A baby should be more than an extension of ourselves
Although at times their parents and other relatives will feel pride,
as their hearts swell.

A baby's existence is not to enhance our popularity
A baby needs consistency, encouragement and positivity.
Not everything a baby does must be exclaimed about
A baby needs the opportunity to explore, to learn and to find out.

Caring for a baby will not always be easy
They will get sick, become fretful and cause their parents a lot of
worries.

But the hope, the joy, the pride and the exciting journey ahead
Is something most parents' treasure, and confront without any
dread.

The strong emotions most people experience when they gaze upon
a baby's face
Accounts for the general excitement and profound hope in the
human race.

What is a baby but a beautiful human being?
Whose miraculous existence warms the soul, and makes the heart
sing.

Babies are a sign of continuity
They have the power to create family unity.
A baby makes everyone feel so cosy
Even when you are aware that their entire life will not always be
rosy!

ADVICE TO TEENAGERS

Dear teenager I think it is important for you to know
Several truths as you mature and grow
Life is full of many twists and turns
And in order to negotiate them you will have to learn.

From the day you were born you feel the love and care that
surrounds you
First of all, from your parents and later on from the extended
family too
Then you go out into the wider world
And your whole horizon and personality begins to unfurl.

You go to school and perhaps even nursery
Before you start your education in primary
Your socialisation will have just begun
And you start to make friends and your world expands.

You start to go from strength to strength
As your knowledge gets greater and your learning becomes more
intense
You now begin to make new choices
As your social life begins to expand and you listen to different
voices.

You are now in secondary school
And you try not to be taken for a fool
You decide which subjects are your strongest
And these are the ones you choose for your tests.

The exam results have all come out
And when you saw your grades you began to laugh and shout
You did a lot better than you had expected
And felt good about the subjects you had selected.

Now you can look further into the future
You might even need to get a new computer
Should you take a break and work or go straight on to college
Have you learnt enough or do you want to increase your
knowledge?

I know that by now you will be frowning because you won't like
some of the things, I have to mention
But I will be failing in my duty if I didn't point you in the right
direction
Life's paths can sometimes be rocky and it is my intention
To tell you some of the things which will help you to make
morally right decisions.

Some of your friends will have done brilliantly whilst others will
not have done so well
What they have in their individual minds it might be hard to tell
Because they are really not giving much away
But you have to be strong and stay focussed so that you are not
easily swayed.

The decisions they make will determine their destinations
And they might want to get there without too much
procrastination
Money might be the thing that for some is most important

And they may well look to you for some sort of endorsement.

But you have to be wise and you have to be smart
And decide whether you're going to use your brains and follow
your heart
I know it will be hard to take a different path from your friends
But in the long run it will be on your own self you will have to
depend.
Your mind had been set on going to university
A decision which takes on great enormity
Many of your friends have decided to take a sabbatical
A decision which you think is rather radical.

Do you follow them or do you follow your own path?
That is the question that has to be asked
What is to be gained by bucking the trend
And doing what is best for you than to try to impress your friends.

There will be lots of parties and social gatherings
And many of your friends will be boastful and swaggering
But you have to decide if that scene is for you
Are these the sorts of things you really want to do?

If you stick to your plans you could become unpopular
You might find yourself becoming insular.
The hardest thing may be to make an informed choice
But it is important to be still and listen to your sensible inner
voice.

How will you be affected by the decisions you make
Which is the best road you will need to take?

What will be the outcome and the consequence?
Exactly what will you have to do to make a difference?

You will see some of your peers drinking and taking drugs
Some of them might even become gang members and thugs
I cannot be with you every hour of the day
So, I am trying to teach you so you do not lose your way.

Maybe you will be tempted to have the experience
So, with drink and drugs you might experiment
I cannot honestly tell you not to try it out
Because I know if you don't, you will always wonder what the
hype is all about.

Be aware that I am not sanctioning you drinking or taking drugs
Because I think people who do those things are mugs
I am just pointing out to you the many temptations
That are around and I feel it is important that we have this
conversation.

Many of your friends will feel the very same as you
But you all have to be very careful of what you do
At your age it is not unusual for you to experiment
But over experimentation could be to your detriment.

So, my dear teenage what I would like to see happen
Is that every time you are tempted to do wrong you will feel
saddened
You will remember what I have said and the sound of my voice
will always be in your head

As I've tried to teach you good morals and I hope you will make the right choices and you will not end up dead.

Ultimately it is up to you how your future pans out
As you go through life you will make some mistakes of that there is no doubt
But if you use life's lessons to conduct yourself in ways that are wise
Will determine whether you will live a life of goodness and pleasure or one of regrets and strife.

So, go my dear teenager, go and fly the nest
I have done my best to educate you and now you must do the rest
Work hard but also live the best life that you can
Go with my love and my blessing because no matter what you do, I will always remain your beloved gran.

THE LIES

There were about thirty of them in the class that day
All falling over themselves as well as each other to say
How their home lives were perfect and serene
And how they were not brought up under the restriction of
"children should only be seen".

Not one of them confessed that they were told they should not be
heard
They just followed each other and they could not be deterred
Everyone had their hand waving in the air shouting 'me miss, me
miss'
Not one of them had the common sense to desist.

The new inexperienced teacher smiled at each one in turn
And wondered how long it would take these children to learn
That the louder they shout is the more they will be ignored
Of this kind of behaviour, they have to be cured.

She changed her tactics and decided to ask
Just a few children who were in the class
But how she would choose them she did not know
Because no favouritism did she want to show.

She moved her gaze around the room
And hoped that inspiration would come soon
Then her eyes lit upon a sullen looking little girl
Whose hair she thought could do with a good comb and maybe a
curl.

Pointing to the little girl she asked her to stand
That definitely made the little girl feel ever so grand
She proudly looked around before she got to her feet
And stood there looking very mild and meek.

Who combed your hair? the teacher asked
And that strange question made the whole class gasp
My auntie combed it she answered boldly
Looking very frightened before bowing her head demurely.

Well your auntie is a wicked woman, the teacher loudly
proclaimed
And she tried very hard to quell the laughter that erupted, but that
was in vain
The poor little girl hung her head in embarrassment
At her classmates' obvious delight and their merriment.

Your auntie had no right to send you looking like that out of the
house
The teacher in a haughty voice announced
Did she not see that your plaits we sticking up in the air instead of
lying down?
Was her intention to turn you into the classroom clown?

Immediately the teacher saw what she had done
As all control of the class was now gone
The unfortunate child was now sobbing quietly
As she had lost all sense of self-worth and dignity.

How do I address this situation the teacher pondered
As again her eyes around the room began to wander
Then she picked on the most fragile looking little boy
Change tactics, she thought, that has got to be my ploy.

Now, who do you live with, how many of you are in your house?
The boy looked around but kept as silent as a mouse
Come on, the teacher urged in a kindly voice
And the silent little boy felt that he had no choice.

I live with my mother and my sisters and granny
He thought he had better reduce it as he didn't want it to sound too
many
And do you get enough to eat? the teacher asked
Making the boy's face shut down as if he was wearing a mask.

Well do speak up so that we can all hear
This is a class where we have discussions and people share
If you like, I can start by telling you what I had for my dinner
Though I must cut that out, as I need to be thinner.

All the children's attention was now on the teacher
And as she spoke their curiosity got deeper
The girl and boy who a while ago felt themselves the centre of
attention
Sighed with great relief at their unexpected redemption.

The teacher reeled off some mouth-watering dish
The children listened in awe as they all wished
That their meagre meals could have contained even one bit of hers
And those who had had nothing at all felt even worse.

Well I had the best dinner last night one boy said
Those who felt bowed down now lifted up their heads
They all waited with bated breaths,
And looked at the speaker with renewed interest.

I had so much food last night my belly almost burst
And loads of nice things to drink to quench my thirst
Another one quickly took up the story
And soon all the children in the class were talking about their food glory.

My belly was full right up to my neck
I didn't stop eating until my mother came to check
My plate was too full I couldn't eat it all
So with my stuffed belly, to my bed I had to crawl.

My dinner was rice and peas and chicken
Mine was pumpkin soup with a lot of dumplings
Mine was fried plantain and steamed fish
All of the children called out their favourite dish.

I was really saddened because I knew the truth
And all these myths I had to diffuse
I had to accept my part in all this
As I searched my mind to change tactics.

I knew the poverty in which these children existed
And felt ashamed at what I had instigated
I know that their parents and carers did their best
To help the children to have enough food and plenty of rest.

But to be poor is an awful thing
It leaves you consistently wondering,
And as I listened to the stories that the children told
My own childhood in my mind began to unfold.

I am now a teacher and I should know better
I should be a role model and a positive role setter
As the tears welled up in my eyes
I confessed to the children that I had lied.

A new bond had formed between myself and my class
As we agreed to be honest with one another at last
Many of them went to bed with only some bread or some porridge
But they were grateful because they knew that that was all their
parents could manage.

I was a big woman and therefore had no excuse
So the tension in the room I decided to diffuse
I changed my story from the banquet I had described
to the truth which I hope they will believe,
That my dinner last night was nothing more than just plain bun
and cheese.

SOCIAL DISTANCING

Social distancing to me is not the phrase to use
Physical distancing is much more meaningful
For the first time neighbours are beginning to know neighbours
And that is the great benefit of this situation.

In the world that we know today
There's a lot of realisation that kindness pays
Volunteers are going about
Giving of their time by helping out.

Those people who are most vulnerable
Are getting assistance which is invaluable
And it would be great that when this pandemic is over
People will continue to treat one another with kindness and
favour.

COVID-19 has made people realise
How important it is to have others in their lives
Through phone calls and zooming plus other means of connecting
They continue to socialise and new friendships are blossoming.

When we meet, we are encouraged to stay two meters apart
It's so hard not to hug and it breaks our hearts
But if we are to stop this virus from spreading
We must observe the rules though some tears we are shedding.

As we gradually come out of lockdown
A new sense of normality has to be found
So, whether it is physical or social distancing
We will breathe a sigh of relief that the isolation is ending.

UNFOUNDED FEAR

I heard the piercing scream and went running into the room
I hardly got inside before I was almost tripped over by the broom
My young sister was standing on top of a chair
With both her arms frantically waving in the air.

I could not tell what it was all about
She was incoherent with her shout
I could not understand a word she said
As she was waving her arm about, pointing and hitting her head.

There, there it is she screamed
And look as I might there was nothing to be seen
What are you pointing at what is the matter?
Before I could move, she jumped off the chair which fell with a
clatter.

She bolted through the open door
And bounded down to the first floor
Still screaming on top of her voice
Making the most appalling noise.

Then there was a persistent ring on the doorbell
There was so much commotion it was hard to tell
Exactly what was transpiring
As all at once everyone was blabbering.

Then into this mix came my ten-year-old nephew
Wanting to know what was the issue

From the secret grin I saw on his face
I bundled him out of the room with indecent haste.

What did you do to give your mum such a fright?
If you know what's good for you you'll get out of her sight
But before you go I'd like to know
What you did to frighten her so.

In the meantime the neighbour was arguing loudly
There must have been some abuse going on it sounded so ugly
She was saying that it was her civic duty to inform the police
But she didn't want to do anything in haste that could cause
malice.

Just then my nephew returned to the scene
I will never understand how some little boys could act so mean
He had in his hand a piece of paper covering a glass
And his face was set as if he was wearing a mask.

In front of us all he unleashed his prize
And everyone was startled by his mother's cries
She sprinted off at great speed like Usain Bolt
But with arms and legs flaying she looked more like a young colt.

My nephew laughed so much he was rolling on the floor
As he saw his mother fly through the door
I must confess that until today I had no idea
That my usually very confident sister was so terrified of a little
spider.

THE GIFT

I woke up with great excitement on this my special day
As time passed, I knew that friends and family were on their way
There was going to be a great celebration
As it was meticulously planned with a lot of deliberation.

As the hours rolled by, I could hardly wait
I had dressed too early which made it seem that everyone was late
I paced up and down and constantly looked out
For goodness sake, sit down and relax, I could hear my best
friend shout.

They will all be there at the time that was planned
Your impatience is really getting out of hand
Since you're in such a hurry, come let's go to the hall
I know we'll be far too early we really should wait for the call.

I knew that what my friend said was true
But when you don't want it to, time always flew
Today was such an important day for me
My friends and family I desperately wanted to see.

Reluctantly I resumed my seat
I took off the shoes that were beginning to hurt my feet
I hastily looked around for some distraction
And my eyes lit on my work out contraption.

My eyes slowly moved around the room
As I fervently hoped that the time would come soon

When all the people I love can gather together
As the sight of them would give me so much pleasure.

Yes, I'm looking forward to seeing them
Maybe that's from where my impatience stem
But I must confess I'm also hoping to get some nice presents
Although I don't want the reason for the celebration to lose its essence.

My main intention was to have a huge gathering
So that we can get together, catch up and listen to all the chattering
It's been a long time since we've done anything like this
I'm really hoping that it all runs smoothly and nothing goes amiss.

At long last the time for the celebration is near
I know that I will be greeted with an ear-splitting cheer
Hurray, the taxi is now at the door
Come on, because the tooting of the horn we can no longer ignore.

Finally, we have arrived at our destination
To rush out of the car was my first inclination
But before I could even rise from my seat
My friend was already out the door and in the street.

I really do not understand how she could have been so quick
She must have been practising for a long time and found a new trick
I excitedly followed her into the hall
And looked forward to having a fantastic ball.

The hour of reckoning has come at last
And the hall was full, I could see from my first glance
As I smiled and waved and greeted the crowd
They clamoured and waved back and shouted my name out loud.

A splendid few hours had been passed
As people gossiped, sang and laughed
The dancing was great and most invigorating
And as the night wore on, my excitement was mounting.

Time for the presents I heard someone announce
Come on, come on, let's start giving them out
As people lined up with their various tokens
There was silence as not a word was spoken.

Everyone waited with bated breaths
To see which present I would think was the best
I thanked each giver and tried to show my sincere gratitude
To everyone who was present in that room.

At last, the long line was coming to an end
Only two people were left, including my best friend
The other person was a little boy
Who had in his hand his favourite toy.

I was moved with joy and immense pleasure
As he greeted me and handed me his treasure
"I knew it was your special day so I looked around
And I've given you the very best thing that I have found".

I lifted the little boy into my arms
And marvelled at his sincerity and his charm
As we danced around, I told him I could never have wished
For anything better than his lovely, special and precious gift.

About the Author

Doreen is a woman of Jamaican heritage living in London. She started writing poetry after seeing the video showing the horrific death of George Floyd- hence the title of her book. Her poems tell stories which are lyrical, stimulating and haunting. They span a wide range of subjects which realistically explore the experiences of peoples' past, their present, and also look at what the possibilities could be in the future.

Doreen was encouraged to publish her poetry by a number of friends and acquaintances. She would especially like to thank her brother-in-law Carlton, her friends Elaine and Jackie, as well as members of the Caribbean Social Forum (which is a social club for mainly people from the Caribbean, but a club which embraces the richness people from all cultures and ethnicity brings). Attendees of this club have read her poems and have given her positive feedback and encouragement.

A special thanks also to her daughter Medina and granddaughter Keira who gave her invaluable help with the technology

Printed in Great Britain
by Amazon